The
Renaissance
of Roman
Architecture

England

HACKER ART BOOKS, INC. NEW YORK, 1975

The RENAISS-ANCE of

Part Two. England

SIR
THOMAS
GRAHAM
JACKSON

Roman
Architecture

First published 1922
Reprinted by permission of Cambridge University Press.

Reissued 1975 by
Hacker Art Books, Inc.
New York.

Library of Congress Catalogue Number 79-143354
ISBN 0-87817-091-X

Printed in the United States of America.

THE RENAISSANCE OF ROMAN ARCHITECTURE

BY

Sir THOMAS GRAHAM JACKSON, Bart., R.A.

Hon. D.C.L. Oxford, Hon. LL.D. Cambridge
Hon. Fellow of Wadham College, Oxford
Associé de l'Académie Royale
de Belgique
F.S.A.

PART II. ENGLAND

Turpe etiam illud est, contentum esse id consequi quod imiteris.
Nihil autem crescit sola imitatione.

QUINTIL. lib. x. cap. 2.

CAMBRIDGE
AT THE UNIVERSITY PRESS
1922

S. PAUL'S CATHEDRAL

From Birch's *London Churches* (Batsford & Co.)

PREFACE

IN the volume forming Part I. of the history of *The Renaissance of Roman Architecture* I followed the history of the movement in Italy. The present volume carries the story onwards to our own country, where the style had a harder fight than elsewhere with the existing native art, and consequently took a special form which distinguishes it from the Renaissance in other lands.

The older style influenced its successor from first to last; and though the most important buildings conformed more or less regularly to the Palladian model, the Gothic art lingered in humbler work, and cannot be said to have quite expired till the Gothic revival, by substituting worship of the letter for the spirit, finally quenched it.

The Gothic revival however was the great artistic event of the nineteenth century, and in spite of its faults and mistakes it led indirectly to the emancipation of the artist from stale convention. Even those who most deplore it have been affected by it, and work in a very different way from what they would have done had it never happened.

The subject of the English Renaissance has been so thoroughly and in a sense exhaustively dealt with by other writers that there seems scarcely room for another book about it. The splendid volumes of Messrs Garner and Stratton on the Tudor Architecture with which it began; those of Mr Gotch on the early, and of Messrs Belcher and Macartney on the later period of the style; and Sir Reginald Blomfield's two volumes on the *History of the Renaissance in England*, with other works, of which I have been glad to avail myself, would seem to have covered the whole field. My contribution to the subject is taken from a rather different point of view; I have tried, as in my previous volumes on Byzantine and

Romanesque Architecture, and on the Gothic period, to explain the movement by the social history of the age, and to show how one reflects the other.

The interval of time since the publication of the first part, treating of the Renaissance in Italy, makes the present volume to some extent an independent work, though the two are intended to be read together. This has involved a certain amount of repetition for which this must be my excuse.

The examples chosen for illustration are such as seemed typical of the art in its successive stages, and I have taken them for choice from monuments with which I have happened to be most familiar, and in some cases professionally connected. Of the original drawings two are by my son Basil; the rest are from my own sketches. The chronological tables at the end of the book will I trust be found useful.

I have to acknowledge my obligations to Mr Stratton and his publishers Messrs Batsford for leave to reproduce Plate II from the book by the late Mr Garner and himself on the *Domestic Architecture of England during the Tudor period*; to Mr Gotch for Plate XXXVII, and Figures 17, 21 and 22 from his *Renaissance Architecture in England*, also published by Messrs Batsford; to the Editor of *Country Life* for Plates IV and V; and to Messrs Batsford for the Plate of St Paul's Cathedral from Birch's *London Churches*.

Finally, I have to thank my friend the Rev. George Horner for kindly reading the proofs, and the University Press for their care in the production of these volumes during a period of difficulty.

T. G. J.

EAGLE HOUSE, WIMBLEDON,
Sept. 6, 1921

CONTENTS

LIST OF ILLUSTRATIONS

ERRATUM

Page 69. For *Contribution* read *Architecture*.

THE ENGLISH RENAISSANCE

CHAPTER I

INTRODUCTION

THE introduction of the Roman styles into English architecture cannot be called a Renaissance in the sense in which we speak of the movement in Italy. It was not the new birth, the revival of a decayed and almost forgotten art that had once lived on our soil. England had indeed during the four hundred years of Roman occupation been covered with Roman buildings, some of them of imposing dimensions, and in tolerably regular Classic style; though there was nothing here comparable to the buildings in Provence, which are equal to those of Italy. But the art of Rome had never become vernacular among the British population. Even in the towns the people were only superficially Italianized, and when the Romans went all traces of Italian culture soon faded away. Though we read that the ambition of the Saxons, when they settled down and felt the need of an architecture, was to build in the manner of the Romans, their idea of building *more Romanorum* came to little more than building in stone instead of in turf and wood, *more Scottorum*.

The Romans in Britain

There was then no sentiment, there were no historical memories to recommend the change when the Classic infection reached our shores. Nor was there a single vestige of Roman architecture visible in our island important enough to serve as a model and inspire imitation. Even in Italy where there was everything to remind the people

No sentiment in England for Roman Art

Tenacity
of Gothic of a great past with which Classic architecture was associated, the Renaissance was not a spontaneous movement
from within, and in several places especially at Milan,
Venice and Bologna, the art of the Middle Ages held its own
for some time and was not abandoned without reluctance[1].
Here as in Italy the change was due to the pressure of
Humanism, and the patronage of royal and noble *dilettanti*;
it was not a natural development from the art of the day,
but a new departure unconnected with what was then
being practised : the introduction of the new art was not
the work of the artists, but of those who employed them,
and forced it upon them.

Revival of
Learning
preceded
that of Art   In England, as in Italy, the Revival of learning, the
literary Renaissance, preceded the artistic Renaissance
and paved the way for it, and it was from Italy that
England like the rest of Europe received the impulse
towards classical studies which led ultimately to the revival
of Roman architecture.

The revival
of learning
due to Italy   "We have the greatest reason to doubt," says the
historian of literature, "whether without the Italians of
those ages it—(the revival of learning)—would ever have
occurred. The trite metaphors of light and darkness, of
dawn and twilight are used carelessly by those who touch
on the literature of the middle ages, and suggest by analogy
an uninterrupted progression, in which learning, like the
sun, has dissipated the shadows of barbarism. But with
closer attention it is easily seen that this is not a correct
representation ; that taking Europe generally, far from
being in a more advanced stage of learning at the beginning of the fifteenth century than two hundred years
before, she had in many respects gone backwards, and
gave little sign of any tendency to recover her ground.

[1] v. Part I. of this work, pp. 23, 61, 75, 87, 165.

There is in fact no security, so far as the past history of mankind assures us, that any nation will be uniformly progressive in science, arts, and letters ; nor do I perceive, whatever may be the current language, that we can expect this with much greater confidence of the whole civilized world[1]."

The influence of Italy on English manners, and more particularly on English literature, goes back to the 14th century, when our language had at last been regularly formed out of its Anglo-Saxon and Norman-French constituents. Chaucer was born in 1328 only 7 years after the death of Dante, and he grew up while Petrarch and Boccaccio were already revolutionizing Italian learning. In 1373 Chaucer was in Italy at Florence and Genoa. Petrarch speaks of meeting him and being promised some information about England which he never received. His visit to Italy confirmed Chaucer in his appreciation of Italian literature. His mastery of the language is proved by his translations[2], and his acquaintance with the great Italian poets by his references to Dante, and by the Canterbury tales, where the stories told by the Knight, the Franklin, and the Shipman are taken from Boccaccio, while that of the patient Griselda is amplified and versified from the last tale in the Decameron. It became the fashion for young men of quality to travel in Italy. The elder Sir Thomas Wyatt and the Earl of Surrey went there early in the 16th century and studied Italian poetry. Wyatt introduced the sonnet and Surrey blank verse into

Italian influence on English literature

Chaucer

Wyatt and Surrey

---

[1] Hallam, *Literature of Europe*, vol. I. p. 126.

[2] Professor Henry Morley says that sixteen stanzas of the *Assembly of Foules* "are translated in a way that places beyond question Chaucer's knowledge of Italian. The turns of phrase make it quite evident that Chaucer wrote with the Italian original before him." *A first sketch of English Literature*, p. 120.

Wyatt and
Surrey England, from Italian models. An old writer of 1589 says
that "having tasted the sweet and stately measures and
style of Italian poetry, as novices crept out of the schools
of Dante, Arioste, and Petrarch, they greatly polished our
rude and homely manner of vulgar poesy[1] from that it
had been before, and for that cause may justly be said to
be the first reformers of our English metre and style[2]."
Thomas Smith, Provost of Eton in the time of Edward VI,
took a Doctor's degree at Padua. Translations from the
Classics began to appear. The whole of Ovid's *Metamorphoses* were translated by Golding between 1565 and
1575. Classical legends became popular, and the Bishop's
Bible of 1566 is embellished with wood-cut initials illustrating Ovid's *Metamorphoses*, including the loves of
Leda and the Swan.

Roger Ascham, who taught Greek to Lady Jane Grey,
complains that books translated from the Italian are sold
in every shop in London, which do more harm by enticing
young men to evil ways than ten sermons at Paul's cross
would do them good by moving them aright. He de-
precates the fashion of sending young men to Italy, and
quotes the Italian saying *Inglese Italianato, diavolo in-
carnato*. He pays a tribute of praise to Castiglione's
Cortegiano; and says that young gentlemen would get
more good from a year's study of that book at home than
from three years spent in Italy. Some writers even trace
a physical likeness between the Italians and the English.
Polydore Vergil says that "as in the sound of their language the English are very like the Italians, so in bodily
habit and manners there is scarcely any difference between
them[3]." That strange genius Girolamo Cardano of Pavia

*English transla-
tions of the
Classics*

*Ascham
and Italian
literature*

*Polydore
Vergil*

*Girolamo
Cardano*

[1] I.e. poetry in the vulgar tongue.   [2] H. Morley, *op. cit.* p. 285.
[3] *Anglicae Historiae Libri vigintisex*, Lib. I.

who visited the court of Edward VI, says the English Resemblance of English to Italians dress like the Italians, "for they are glad to boast themselves nearly allied to them, and therefore study to imitate as much as possible their manner and their clothes. Certain it is that all the barbarians of Europe love the Italians more than any race among themselves." He goes on to say that "perhaps they do not know our wickedness[1]."

It is hardly necessary to say how much Shakespear Shakespear owed to Classic and Italian story. In ten of his plays the characters and generally the scene are drawn from Italy.

If the study of the Classics, *litterae humaniores*, was Early study of the Classics in England not at first pursued in England by the cultivated classes generally with the same avidity as in Italy, it was at all events not far behind in point of date. The translation of Cicero *de Amicitia*, by Tiptoft, Earl of Worcester, is coeval with the invention of printing with moveable type; and in 1491, the year before the death of Lorenzo de Medici, William Grocyn, who had been in Italy, and had learned Greek from Demetrius Chalcondylas, settled at Study of Greek Oxford as the first teacher of that language. He was followed by Linacre and Lily. In 1497 Erasmus, hearing Erasmus, More and Colet that Oxford was one of the few places where Greek was taught, came thither and not only learned it, but was welcomed by Greek scholars with whom he formed enduring friendships. Sir Thomas More wrote Greek

---

[1] Elsewhere Cardano says: "When I was in England, and rode about on horseback in the neighbourhood of London, I seemed to be in Italy. When I looked among those groups of English sitting together I completely thought myself to be among Italians: they were like, as I said, in figure, manners, dress, gesture, colour, but when they opened their mouth I could not understand so much as a word, and wondered at them, as if they were my countrymen gone mad and raving. For they inflect the tongue upon the palate, twist words in their mouth, and maintain a sort of gnashing with their teeth." From the *Dialogus de Morte*, H. Morley, *Life of Girolamo Cardano*, vol. II. p. 145.

epigrams, and Dean Colet the founder of S. Paul's school directs in the statutes of 1518 that the master, "if such can be gotten," should know Greek and teach it to the boys. Indeed it is said that during the reign of Leo X, "the Cisalpine nations were gaining ground on their brilliant neighbour."

Italy fre-quented by English

The influence of classical studies on the introduction of classical architecture was no doubt considerable, but the main impulse seems to have been given by a closer acquaintance with Italy, and association with Italians. The noblemen who visited Italy in the reign of Henry VIII would have seen the palaces by Brunelleschi, Da Majano, Michellozzi, Alberti and others at Florence, the villas of

Effect on them of Italian re-finement

the Medici at Careggio and Caffagiuolo, the palaces at Venice, Urbino, Pienza, Milan, and Rome, and in all the great cities of that country, built with a splendour, and furnished with a degree of luxury, comfort, and refinement

Social habits in England

unknown to them at home. In England they still ate with their fingers, holding the meat in the left hand and cutting it with a knife in the right. Tom Coryat travelling in Italy as late as 1608 was surprised to see people eating with forks. He does not think that "any other nation of Christendome doth use it (this custom) but only Italy." In France well-bred people are told in the latter part of the 17th century "*porter la viande à la bouche avec sa fourchette*," but it was the 18th century before forks were generally in use. When Charles II entertained the Duke of Tuscany there were forks, perhaps a concession to Italian prejudices[1]. Erasmus speaks of earthen floors strewn with rushes which were seldom changed, and became foul with scraps from the tables, exhaling at

[1] Warrack, *Domestic Life in Scotland*, p. 192. Compare the *Loseley household accounts* and Maxwell Lyte's *History of Dunster*.

changes of weather odours which he considered unwhole-
some[1]. In the inventories of household stuff that have been
preserved it is surprising to find with what slender furniture
our ancestors were satisfied—tables on tressels, and forms
for everyone but the master, who had the only chair.
When James IV of Scotland entertained his affianced bride
Margaret Tudor, sister of Henry VIII, we read " The
Kynge satt in the Chayre and the Quene abooffe hym on
hys ryght haund. For because the Stole of the Quene
was not for hyr ease he gaffe hyr the sayde Chayre." This
was thought an extraordinary piece of courtesy[2]. Beds
and bedding were precious articles and were made the
subjects of special bequests by will and testament. Thomas
Sackville, Lord Buckhurst, poet and author of *Gorboduc*
the first English tragedy, when required to receive the
Cardinal of Chatillon and his attendant bishop with their
train in his house at Shene, had to borrow table linen and
bedding, and to lend the Cardinal his own bason and
ewer and go without himself; while Lady Buckhurst's
waiting-women had to sleep on the floor that the "Bushup"
might have their bedstead. Eighteen years earlier Sir
Thomas Hoby describes his very different entertainment
by an Italian nobleman at Salerno, who lodged him in a
chamber "hanged with cloth of gold and vellute with
furniture of silver, and bedding embroidered curiously with
needlework." In the Palace at Urbino may be seen bath-
rooms and even contrivances for supply of hot water[3].

It was natural that when the barbarians, as Cardano
calls them, returned to their English homes from a visit
to Italy they were struck with the contrast between the
style of living here and there, even in spite of the great

---

[1] Dr Boorde, an eminent physician, recommends a plaster of this filthy
trodden earth as a useful application in certain complaints.

[2] Warrack, *op. cit.* p. 107.   [3] v. my *Holiday in Umbria*, p 95.

Improve-
ment in
civil archi-
tecture
under the
Tudors
improvement that had already taken place in our domestic architecture. The houses of the Tudor period were indeed far superior in point of domestic comfort to those of the preceding ages. When England settled down in tranquillity after the Wars of the Roses, and the country was no longer vexed by private wars, and civil commotions, men breathed more freely, and began to house themselves after a different fashion. They crept forth from their gloomy donjons with slits for light, and opened large traceried windows in their ancient walls. They threw

House
unfortified
down the fortifications no longer needed for safety, and let air and sunshine into their homes, retaining at most the protection of a moat, which for a time survived the other castellated defences. Ralph Lord Cromwell, who

Tattersall
built Tattersall Castle between 1433 and 1455, with all the defences of a feudal fortress, began as soon as he had

S. Wing-
field
finished it to build the manor house of South Wingfield which was unfortified, and is perhaps the earliest example of a courtyard mansion[1]. The change began earliest

College
buildings
within the walls of cities, as at our Universities, where the type of building for academic life was settled once for all by William of Wykeham in 1380; for when we build Colleges now we still build them on his model. The chambers had fireplaces, and were convenient and airy. The same liberal allowance of space was given in such buildings as the Hospital of S. Cross near Winchester, though that is to some extent protected by walls and a gateway tower, not being within the city defences.

Type of
the manor
house
The planning of the Tudor house was very simple, and the same arrangement of the principal rooms was so generally followed that like the disposition of the parts

[1] He sold it to the Earl of Shrewsbury, who occupied it in 1458. It is now a ruin.

of a convent it may almost be said to have been stand- Plan of
the Tudor
House
ardized. It was specified in 1547 by Andrew Boorde or
"Andreas Perforatus," the witty physician of Henry VIII,
as follows[1]:

> "Make the hall vnder such a fasshyon that the parler be anexed
> to the heade of the Hall; and the buttrye and pantrye be at the
> lower ende thereof. The seller vnder the pantrye sette somwhat
> abase, the kychen sett somewhat a base from the buttrye and pantrye,
> commyng with an entry by the wall of the buttrye; the pastrie-howse
> and the larder-howse anexed to the kychen. Than devyde the
> lodgynges by the cyrceute of the quadrynyall courte, and let the
> gate-howse be opposyt or agaynst the hall-dore not dyrectly, but
> the hall-dore standing a base and the gatehowse in the mydle of the
> front entrynge into the place: let the pryue chambre be anexed to Domestic
plan stand-
ardized
> the chambre of astate, with other chambres necessarye for the
> buyldynge, so that many of the chambres may haue a prospecte in
> to the chapell."

These directions are followed closely in the plan of
SLAUGHAM PLACE (Fig. 1, p. 10). The principal living
room was the Hall with a dais and a high table at the upper The Hall
end, behind which was the withdrawing room to which the
family and their principal guests retired. At the lower end
was a screen, and above it in important houses, a minstrel's
gallery. Doors in the screen admitted to a cross passage
which was entered from the courtyard, and opposite was
the buttery, and a door to the kitchen offices. This, which The offices
was the usual type of a manor house is to be seen still in
the colleges at Oxford and Cambridge. There is little
difference between John Thorpe's plan for SLAUGHAM
PLACE (Fig. 1) and that of Wadham College at Oxford
(Fig. 39, p. 128).

Dr Boorde's is of course the specification for a larger
manor house, built round a quadrangular court, the plan
inherited from the castle of earlier days. But in the smaller

[1] *A compendyous Regyment or a dyetary of Helth made in Mountpyllier,
compyled by Andrew Boorde of Physycke Doctour.*

houses, consisting of simple blocks of building, the same arrangement of the principal rooms was observed in the main, with minor differences occasioned by local conditions.

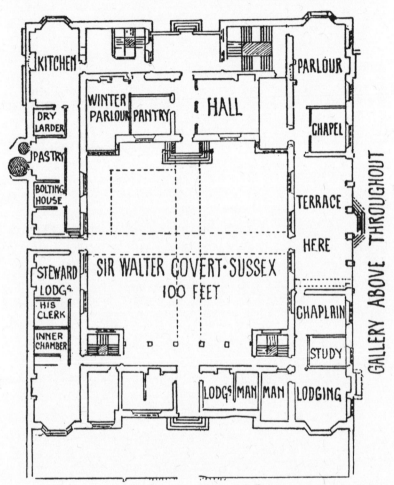

Fig. 1. Slaugham Place. (Adapted from Thorpe.)

Except in the arrangement of the principal rooms there was little attempt at any regularity of plan in the earlier manor houses. At Great Chalfield Manor House,

Wiltshire, built towards the end of Henry VII's reign, the front finishes with a gable at each end, with an oriel window in each, but the two oriels are deliberately made unlike one another[1]. Generally however there was no pretence of symmetry at all. In the earlier colleges older than the 17th century the Hall and Chapel are placed irregularly on

Chalfield Manor

Symmetry disregarded

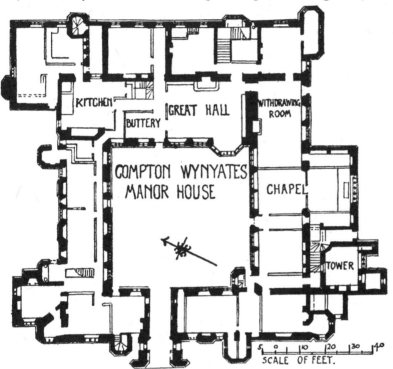

Fig. 2. (Adapted from Garner and Stratton.)

one side of the quadrangle or even outside it. At S. Cross the entrance tower is in one corner of the court. In the private manor houses with an interior court, like Ightham Mote, and COMPTON WYNYATES (Fig. 2), the different parts

Ightham and Compton Wynyates

[1] v. Garner and Stratton, *Tudor Architecture*, vol. I. Illustrations of the other buildings here mentioned as of this period will be found in their two fine volumes.

Irregular
planning seem to have come together by accident, and the same, with some modification, may be said of Cowdray and Hengrave Hall, though at the latter an attempt is made to attain a symmetrical front by extending a wing with nothing behind it beyond the main quadrangular block of the house. In those houses that have no interior courts such as South Wraxall, Parnham Manor in Dorset, East Barsham, and many more, irregularity is the rule. Sutton Place in Surrey is an early instance of a manor house laid out on a regular symmetrical plan from the first (Fig. 9, p. 39).

Symmetry
and the
Renais-
sance Symmetry and Classical architecture are generally supposed to go together, but there is no reason to suppose that the early and imperfect attempts at symmetry in Tudor buildings were the result of any influence exerted by the coming Classical Renaissance. It is natural for any man, when planning a building, to begin symmetrically when there is no reason for doing otherwise. Irregularity in planning is not natural but accidental; occasioned by problems of convenience, or difficulties of site, or other local conditions. In the 17th and 18th centuries symmetry often was insisted upon at the expense of convenience, but in the Gothic period, reasonable considerations happily prevailed, and gave us those delightful and picturesque buildings of which the very irregularities please us, because we can trace a reason for them.

Passing of
the Middle
Ages The change to these irregular and defenceless manor houses from the Castle of the middle ages—from the close fortress that defied and frowned on its neighbours to the open mansion that spoke of genial hospitality—marks the change that began under the Tudors from mediaeval to modern England. The passing of the Feudal Castle meant the end of feudalism, the decline of the old nobility, and

the rise of new families to take their place. For the Mortimers, the Bohuns, the Bigods, Mowbrays, and Nevilles of the middle ages we find the names of Russell, Cavendish, Seymour, Grey, Dudley, Cecil, Herbert, and Fitzwilliam. The old feudal nobility, which had been a constant check on the royal power, was weakened or destroyed by the Wars of the Roses, and the new nobles were the creatures of the king, subservient to the growing despotism, which reached its height under Henry VIII. It has been observed that all important offices of state, or in the army and navy, were filled by men who had been in personal attendance on the king: the Howards, Brandons, Jerninghams, Sidneys, Sherbornes, Marneys, and Fitzwilliams were, or had all been Squires or Knights of the Body, or gentlemen of the chamber[1]. They were enriched and employed, and way was made for new men from the commonalty like Wolsey and Thomas Cromwell, who were dependent on the breath of their master, and whom he could cast aside or destroy with impunity when he no longer wanted them. Wealth carried it over birth, and the spoils of the monasteries which were poured into the lap of the obedient courtiers enabled them to indulge the passion for splendour both in building and establishment which was characteristic of the age, and of which the king set the example. Henry VIII, "the onlie Phœnix of his time for fine and curious masonrie," built the palaces of Bridewell, Nonsuch, St James's, and Beaulieu[2]: Wolsey built Hampton Court, and began his Colleges at Ipswich and Oxford, besides repairing and improving more than one Episcopal

The new nobility

Their dependence on the Court

The wealth of the Courtiers

---

[1] *Social England*, III. p. 85.

[2] Beaulieu is the name given by him to New-Hall in Essex, near Boreham, which he obtained by exchange with Sir Thomas Boleyn, father of Queen Anne. It bears an inscription, *Henricus octavus rex inclit: struxit hoc opus egregium.*

residence[1]; and noble began to vie with noble in the magnificence and scale of their palaces. Like the older nobility also, the gentry, depressed and impoverished by

The new Squire-archy

civil commotion, made way for the rise of the middle classes, and new families of country squires were founded by opulent merchants, whose dwellings soon began to rival those of the nobles. The rich clothiers of the eastern

Rise of wealthy traders

counties enlarged or rebuilt their fine churches; the names of several are recorded on the walls of Long Melford, inlaid in flint-work; the Springs, clothiers of Lavenham, intermarried with their noble neighbours the de Veres; one of them built and endowed a beautiful chantry-chapel in the church with his name and his wife's in flint-mosaic along the cornice[2]; and in 1525 Sir Thomas Kytson,

Hengrave Hall

citizen and mercer of London, built Hengrave Hall, one of the finest mansions of its date in England.

Such was the state of English Society at the opening of the 16th century. But though a higher culture, a wider outlook, a passion for magnificence, and an accession of wealth, made the upper classes ripe for the change, there

No tend-ency yet towards the Re-naissance

was as yet no approach toward the new Roman archi-tecture which had won the victory in Italy. Till far into the English *cinquecento*, the 16th century, the native Gothic style, continued with little or no sign of any coming change. Among all the countries of western Europe ours was the most persistent in clinging to native tradition; the most reluctant to abandon the art that had grown up with the nation, and seemed an essential part of its history. It was by the way of domestic work, naturally more elastic than

[1] He pleaded that his successor should not charge dilapidations against his executors, as he had spent £30,000 on the archiepiscopal buildings.

[2] Illustrated in my *Gothic Architecture in France, England and Italy*, vol. II. p. 120.

ecclesiastical architecture, that the change crept in. Church building had practically ceased ; no church of importance was begun after the Reformation till near the middle of the 17th century, and as the energies of the architect were devoted to domestic buildings, more favourable opportunities for novelty prevented themselves.

It was now that the influence of the Humanities, the new learning, and the worship of Italian culture, made itself felt. Francis I and Henry VIII both invited Italian artists and Italian craftsmen to their courts, and it is from their hands that we get the first touches of the new art. It was long however before it made any serious impression on the architecture : the early examples of Renaissance work are confined to ornamental details, which are curiously mixed up with Gothic ornament, and applied to Gothic designs, and to tombs in which the foreign architect had a more free hand, though even there the work of the native craftsman occasionally shows itself. The work of these Italian artists, and the influence which they exerted on that of their English fellow-workers forms the first chapter in the history of the Renaissance in England.

CHAPTER II

THE EARLY RENÀISSANCE

ONE of the earliest examples of Italian work in an
English building is to be found at LAYER-MARNEY in
Essex, where early in the 16th century Sir Henry Marney,
of the old family which gave its name to the village,
began to build a sumptuous mansion. It was not fortified,
and made no pretence of any defence ; for there was not
even a moat. The gateway tower and part of the front
alone exist ; the quadrangle which was to have lain behind
does not seem ever to have been built (Plate I).

Sir Henry Marney was one of the courtiers who came
to the front under Henry VIII. He first appears as a
simple esquire, one of a class described by Henry as
" scant well-born gentlemen of no great lands till they
were promoted by us." From the service of Margaret,
Countess of Richmond, the king's grandmother, who made
him one of her executors, he passed into that of the king
who made him a privy councillor, a Knight of the Garter
and Captain of the Guard ; and finally in 1523 he was
raised to the Peerage as Baron Marney, and died in the
same year[1].

LAYER MARNEY TOWER, as the house is generally
called, for the lofty towered gatehouse dominates the rest,
and commands the country around, is built of red brick
with dressings of terra-cotta. As the historian of Essex
says "what appears in it about the windows as stonework
is only white brick earth framed in a mould[2]". The lofty

[1] *Essex Archaeol. Soc. Transactions*, vol. III. part I. p. 14.
[2] Morant, *History of Essex*, 1768.

Plate 1

B. H. J.

LAYER MARNEY

gatehouse has four angle turrets, those to the south front Layer Marney Tower
70 feet high, semi-octagons with eight storeys of windows,
between which are two storeys of large chambers above
the gateway. Westwards stretches a wing containing the
habitable part of the house, and on the East, but detached

Fig. 3.

from the main building, is a vast range of stable and farm The out-buildings
buildings, containing long dormitories, and other apart-
ments. Essex is not a stone county, difficulty of land Scarcity of stone
transport made that material very costly, and the homely
brickwork which was the local material was dressed with

Use of
terra-
cotta

Italians
employed

Renais-
sance
parapet
terra-cotta, which after all is only a glorified brick. Terra-
cotta was brought to perfection in Lombardy, where
stone is as scarce as in Essex, and Italians were employed
for the terra-cotta here and elsewhere in the home counties
of England. The terra-cotta at Layer Marney is excellently modelled in the Renaissance manner, though the
architecture of the building is otherwise in the ordinary
Tudor Gothic style of the date. The towers are crowned
by a cornice decorated with the Classic Guilloche and egg
and dart, though it rests on an arcaded course of trefoil

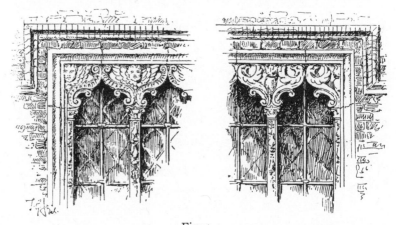

Fig. 4.

cusping which is purely Gothic. Above are grand flourishing battlements with Dolphins and Scrolls (Fig. 3). More
singular is the design of the windows, where the Italian,
Renais-
sance ver-
sion of
window
set to design an ordinary Perpendicular window, has translated it into a queer Renaissance composition which is
very interesting. The mullion is square and flat, and
ornamented down the front with a sort of arabesque, and
it carries an Ionic capital. But the head of the light
evidently puzzled the artist, unfamiliar with the Gothic

cusp, and he has produced what at a distance has something of the same effect, but on a nearer approach is found to consist of scroll-work with cherubs' heads (Fig. 4).

But the Italian work at Layer Marney is not confined to the mansion; the church contains tombs with terracotta of Henry Lord Marney and his son John with whom the title expired. The church is built of brick like the house: even the mullions and arched heads of the windows are in brick cut or moulded to Gothic detail. The chapel which forms a spacious aisle on the north of the Chancel, was begun by Sir Henry Marney and finished apparently after his death. In the will he executed in 1522 the year before his death, when leaving England with Charles Brandon Duke of Suffolk for the invasion of France, he directs "that the chapel he had begun be new made with a substantial roof of timber covered with lead, and the windows to be glazed with imagery. Likewise that a tomb of marble should be made in the wall betwixt the chancel and the same chapel with his image and those of his two wives, Thomasine on his right hand and Elizabeth on his left."

The tomb was accordingly made by his successor under an arch between the chancel and the chapel as he had directed by his will. The effigy is finely carved in black marble; it wears the Garter robes, and lies on a slab of black marble or touch-stone. This forms the top of an altar tomb of which the sides are panelled with terra-cotta displaying the Marney arms within the circle of the Garter. Overhead is a splendid canopy of terra-cotta, supported on panelled and balustraded work at each end, and surmounted with elaborate battlementing recalling that on the towers of the mansion. The whole abounds with

Tomb at
Layer
Marney

Fig. 5.

dolphins, scrolls, wreaths, vases, and candelabra, and all the fantastic devices of the Italian *cinquecento* (Fig. 5). The two ladies do not appear, nor is there room provided for them on the black marble slab.

The North or Marney chapel, to which the fine alabaster tomb of Sir William Marney who died in 1402, and was buried *in choro ecclesiae*, has now been moved, also contains that of John, the second and last Lord Marney. By his will, dated 1524, he directs that he shall be "buried in the midst of the new Isle or Chapel, and the tomb to be of the same stone as his father's, or else of gray marble." He appoints also "an image of brass for himself, and on either side of his image one for each of his two wives." But neither in this case did the ladies receive any recognition, and instead of the three brasses directed to be inlaid on the tomb, Lord John has a black marble effigy of himself like his father lying on a slab of the same touch-stone. The sides of the altar tomb have terra-cotta panels like the other, but there is no canopy. This last Lord Marney died in 1525.

Where was this terra-cotta moulded and baked, and who were these Italians who designed and made it? Dallaway suggests, in his notes to *Horace Walpole*, that "the Layer Marney ornaments were very likely executed under the influence of Girolamo da Trevizi, the king's architect, with whom Sir Henry Marney as Captain of the Guard must have been in continual contact." But Girolamo da Trevigi or Trevisano, was only 16 at the death of Lord Marney, and did not come to England till many years later, towards the end of his career.

It may be added that one of Lord John's wives did after all get her brass, for the effigy of Dame Brygett Marney who died in 1549 lies between those of her two husbands, of whom Lord Marney was the second, in the church of Little Horkesley[1].

In 1515 the Knights Hospitallers leased the estate of

HAMPTON COURT, with their old manor house upon it, to Thomas Wolsey, Archbishop of York, for 99 years at the annual rent of £50. Wolsey had then reached the summit of his ambition. He was Chancellor of the realm, Cardinal, and Papal legate *a latere*. Together with his Arch-bishopric he held the bishopric of Bath and Wells till 1518, when he resigned it to take that of Durham, which he afterwards exchanged for Winchester in 1529. Besides this he was made bishop of Tournay in Flanders, when Henry took that town, and he held *in commendam*, the Abbey of S. Albans and administered the bishoprics of Bath, Worcester, and Hereford, which were held by non-resident foreigners. His wealth was enormous, his power supreme, and the palace which he began to build on his new possession was planned on a regal scale. George

Cavendish, his biographer and faithful gentleman-usher, describes and glories in the splendour of his master's establishment. He had noblemen and gentlemen in waiting, and yeomen in every department, chosen for stature and comeliness. His master cook "went daily in damask, satin, or velvet, with a chain of gold about his neck." For his chapel he had "a Dean, who was always a great scholar and a Divine, a Sub-dean, a Repeater of the quire, a Gospeller, a Pisteller, and twelve singing priests. Of Scholars he had first a Master of the children, twelve singing children, sixteen singing men, with a servant to attend upon the said children[2]." Whenever he went or

[1] *Essex Archaeol. Transactions, op. cit.* p. 31.
[2] *The Life of Cardinal Wolsey,* by George Cavendish, his gentleman usher.

rode abroad, two priests, the tallest and comeliest to be
found within the realm, bore before him two crosses, one
for his archbishopric, and one for his " Legacy." His
domestic establishment amounted to five hundred persons.
Cavendish revels in the account of the display of gold and
silver plate when his master entertained the French
Ambassadors at Hampton Court: it filled six shelves of
a buffet or dresser that occupied the whole end of the
chamber, and he says none of it was stirred during the
feast, for there was enough without it[1]. The furniture was
on an equally lavish scale. There was none of that poverty
which I have alluded to as common in the equipment of
gentlemen's houses at this period, and indeed the clergy
seem always to have lived with much greater comfort
and refinement than the nobility and gentry. The floors
were carpeted, and all the principal chambers were hung
with costly tapestries ; those in the Cardinal's room, says
the Venetian Ambassador, were changed once a week.
There were baths and other sanitary conveniences, and
one of the French envoys, Du Bellay, says, " The very
bed chambers had hangings of wonderful value, and every
place did glitter with innumerable vessels of gold and
silver. There were two hundred and four-score beds, the
furniture to most of them being silk, and all for the entertainment of strangers only[2]." Nothing, it is said, had ever
been seen like it out of Rome.

"Thus," says Cavendish, "passed the Cardinal his life
and time from day to day, and year to year, in such great
wealth, joy, and triumph and glory, having always on his
side the king's especial favour ; until Fortune, of whose

[1] It should be remembered that in those days, when there were no public
stocks in which to invest money, it was customary to invest it in plate and
jewelry as the best securities.

[2] Law, *History of Hampton Court*, pp. 55-111.

favour no man is longer assured than she is disposed,
began to wax somewhat wroth with his prosperous estate,
and thought she would devise a mean to abate his high
part: wherefore she procured Venus, the insatiate goddess
to be her instrument."

But even before Venus, by means of the divorce and
Anne Boleyn, contrived the Cardinal's ruin, the splendour
of Wolsey's new building, far eclipsing Henry's modest
palace at Hanworth a few miles away, provoked his sus-
picious master's jealousy. The story goes that Henry
with signs of displeasure asked the Cardinal why he was
building so magnificent a house at Hampton Court; and
that Wolsey, in alarm, replied "In order to show how
noble a palace a subject may offer to his sovereign." At
all events in 1526 Wolsey made over Hampton Court to
the king with all the furniture, tapestry, and plate that it
contained. He continued however to use the house, and
gave entertainments there till his fall three years later.

The first or "base court" is of Wolsey's building.
The material is brick of a beautiful sober red, with stone
dressings sparingly used, for Middlesex and Surrey are
not stone counties. Although, as we have seen, military
defences were out of date, Hampton Court was defended
by a moat, part of which has lately been exposed. The
entrance is by an archway between two widely spaced
octagonal turrets, and in its present form the composition
is ungraceful, for the part between the turrets seems depressed, and the small octagonal piers that flank the
doorway are unmeaning. It is said that the central part
was originally higher and in better proportion[1]. The
turrets here and elsewhere throughout the building were
originally crowned with "typys" or cupolas, covered with

[1] E. Law, *op. cit.* vol. I. p. 250.

Plate II

HAMPTON COURT

From Garner & Stratton's *Tudor Architecture* (Batsford & Co.)

lead and finished with finials and gilded vanes. All these
have now vanished.

The gateway with four octagonal turrets by which the
second, or Clock Court at Hampton Court is entered is
much more satisfactory. The left side of this quadrangle
is occupied by the Great Hall (Plate II), and the right by
Wolsey's own apartments now hidden from the court by
Wren's colonnade. The Hall is not part of Wolsey's work,
but was built by Henry VIII, who promptly occupied the
palace on Wolsey's disgrace and fall. In the traceries of
the roof his cypher occurs joined with that of Jane Seymour
whom he married in 1536 the day after Anne Boleyn's
head fell on the scaffold. Henry bought the freehold from
the Hospitallers, pulled down Wolsey's Hall and built
the present splendid structure. Other extensive buildings,
the King's Lodgings, and the Queen's for poor Anne
Boleyn, which he added, beyond the palace eastward, were
destroyed by Wren to make way for the state rooms and
fountain court of William and Mary. Henry pushed on
the work at his new Hall with impatience. We read of
men working late "in their owre tymys and drynkyng
tymys, for the hasty expedition of the same." Tallow
candles at 18*d.* the dozen are bought for the carpenters
working after dark "upon the Vought of the kynge's new
Hall." There are payments for " Empcion of bryke " to
William Love of Bronxam in Herts at 4*s.* 6*d.* a thousand
delivered at Taplow on the river, whence they were brought
to the site by water, and to " John Larkyn of Salsryde-
worthe brykmaker, for digging, moulding, settyng and
byrning of five hundryth thousande fourescore three
thousand brykkes by hym byrnt and delyveryd at the
bryk-kills wythin the kynge's parke at Hampton Court,
takyng for every 1000 brykkes thereso brent and de-

The clock court and gateway

The Great Hall

The bricks

lyveryd at 2s. 10d., £82. 11s. 10d." Other bricks therefore

seem to have been made locally. Stone was brought from Caen to S. Katharine's wharf in London, and thence by barges up the river. Firestone for the hearths came from Reigate, lead from Master Babyngton of Derbyshire[1].

The architecture throughout, whether Wolsey's or Henry's, is ordinary Late Perpendicular Gothic, with four-centred arches, lights uncusped except in the great end windows of the Hall, stringcourses, battlements and pinnacles bristling with weather-vanes. The Hall has a

magnificent hammer-beam roof, with the peculiarity of a short cant at the summit which by a sort of queen-post construction cleverly curtails what would have been an excessively high pointed gable. At the upper end is a square oriel with a beautiful ceiling of fan-tracery. It is perhaps the finest Gothic Hall in the kingdom, excepting only that at Westminster.

The chimney shafts are of brick, moulded, diapered, and twisted, in the fantastic fashion of the day. They were made by Robert Burdyes "bryklayer" of Hampton who received £27 for twelve chimney shafts "with their basys, geraunds, and heddes, reddy sett up and fenysshed upon the Queene's new Lodging." They were painted; for 9½ lb. of "verdygrese" is bought "to color chimneys," and "four dozen of red lead for painting them."

In selecting a site for his palace Wolsey took advice of the best physicians as to its healthiness; and in order to

---

[1] Law, op. cit. vol. I. pp. 157–161. In an Appendix he gives a list of the wages paid: Carpenters, 6d. a day, and overtime at the rate of 7d.; Bricklayers, 6d. a day; Freemasons, that is, masons who worked on the free-stone, for doors, windows, coigns for buttresses and "gresse-tables," or steps, 3s. a week; ordinary masons, "Setters or Lodgemen," of whom there were 90 or 100, 3s. 8d. and 3s. 4d. a week, which is higher pay than the freemasons, and I think must be a mistake.

ensure a pure supply of water he brought it from Combe by a conduit of $2\frac{1}{2}$ inch lead pipes, which passed under the river and is calculated to have cost the equivalent of £50,000 of our money[1]. There is no architect named: the priest Mr Williams, mentioned as surveyor of the works, may have been only clerk and paymaster, and John of Padua, that man of mystery, was not appointed "deviser" of Henry's works till 1544 after the Palace had been finished, nor would he have worked in the Gothic style.

Wolsey however showed that he was alive to the fine art then practised in Italy, by employing Italians in some of the decorative details. Let into the octagon turrets that flank both entrances are terra-cotta medallions with busts of Roman emperors, set in hollow discs, surrounded by mouldings of egg and dart, and wreaths of foliage (Fig. 6, p. 28). They are admirably designed and show the deft Florentine or Tuscan hand. The artist, Joannes Majano, was paid £2. 6s. 0d. each for these *rotundae imagines ex terra depictae* for the palace at "Anton Cort." There are also panels of heraldry over the archways in terra-cotta with supporters and other ornamental details; only in one place on the inside of the second gateway has Wolsey's escutcheon escaped, the rest on the outside of that tower and both sides of the other being the royal arms of his master, for carving which Edmund More, freemason of Kingston, was paid £34. 4s. 10d.

Wolsey's arms, which are now borne by Christchurch, the college first founded by him at Oxford, are surmounted by the Cardinal's hat and supported by two winged children, cherubs or *Putti*, and are enclosed in a panel

---

[1] The lead pipes are half an inch thick, and are seamed like the Roman pipes. The amount of lead is said to be 250 tons. The pipe under the Thames was several times broken by the anchor of a barge. Law, *op. cit.* vol. I.

of Renaissance architecture with fluted Corinthian columns, and a regular entablature with swags on the frieze. Above these was originally a shallow lunette with the initials T. W. and the date 1525. This has now disappeared. Whether this Giovanni da Majano, working at Hampton Court about 1520, was related to Benedetto, also of Majano,

Fig. 6.

architect of the Strozzi Palace at Florence, whose amusing adventure with the chests of *intarsiatura* is recorded in my first volume, we are not told[1]. Benedetto died a young man in 1498.

Wolsey's closet

The room shown as Wolsey's closet, though it has a mullioned window, doors, and fireplace of Tudor Gothic,

[1] Part I. *Italy*, p. 140.

is decorated by Italian artists. The ceiling is panelled, Wolsey's
closet
painted and gilt, with renaissance details, and there is a
cornice with a "border of antyke with naked childer, the
antyke alle gylte, the ffylde layde with ffyne byse," or blue,
which though, as Mr Law says, perhaps not originally
belonging to this room, at all events bears Wolsey's motto
Dominus michi adiutor. Below on the upper part of the Italian
painting
walls are paintings of scenes from our Lord's passion,

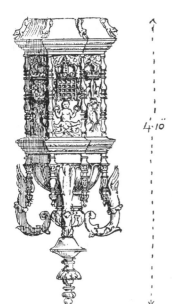

Fig. 7.   Lower pendant.

4·10

3·4

Fig. 8.   Upper pendant.

perhaps by Luca Penni, or Toto della Nunziata, of whom
more by and by[1].

The Renaissance touch in Henry's work appears again
in the pendants of the Hall roof, though all the rest of it The Hall
is regular Gothic work (Figs. 7, 8). In the upper tier pendants

[1] Law, *op. cit.* vol. I. p. 53 and do. p. 363, "Emption of Paynter's stuff
spent by Anthony Tote in the Kynges closett at Hampton Court, Dec. 1532.

there are cherubs holding hands; in the lower and larger
they support heraldic emblems, little balusters form the
angles, and the lower part is finished with vases, and fluted
surfaces. But one finds with surprise that they are the
work of an English artist, and not an Italian. Richard
Rydge of London, " Karver," was paid " for the making
of 16 pendants standing under the hammer beam in the
Kynge's new hall at 3s. 4d. the peece[1]." It would seem
that the native carvers soon caught the infection of the
new art from the Italians who associated with them, and
it is curious to find in the accounts the word *entayling* for
carving, which is evidently the Italian *intagliare*[2].

The names of the workmen employed throughout are
English. Richard Rydge seems to have been the chief
" karver " of the " antyk worke," and the Royal badges ;
but Thomas Johnson of London carved the " Kynge's
beasts" on the battlements and on the femerell or lantern
of the great Hall, at 16s. 8d. a piece. The painting and
gilding was done by John Hethe and Henry Blankston.
John à Guylders, the Smith, alone may perhaps from his
name be a Dutchman. He made the great vane on "the
ffemerall, barying the close crown," for which he was paid
40s.

The outlay on Henry's building was £400 a month,
equal in value to £50,000 a year of our currency. And
Hampton Court was only one of his new palaces. "What
a great charge it is to the king to continue his buildings

---

[1] Law, *op. cit.* vol. I. pp. 173, 354. There seems some confusion here, for
Rydge is paid 25 shillings each for the smaller pendants above the hammer
beams.

[2] " Payd to William Reynoldes fremason for entayling of too crownys in
freston standing over the Kinges armys and the queenys at the Chappell dore
at 5s. the pece." The painting and gilding of the arms cost 20s. each. Law,
op. cit. vol. I. p. 358.

" Here I do behold these entayled images." Cavendish, *Life of Wolsey.*

in so many places at once," says Cromwell in his Reminiscences, "How proud and false the workmen be: and if the king would spare for one year how profitable it would be to him[1]."

NONSUCH PALACE, one of these royal extravagances, which stood between Ewell and Cheam in Surrey, has entirely disappeared. The church, manor house, and village of Cuddington were destroyed to make way for it and for Nonsuch and Worcester parks adjoining. Henry did not finish it, and it was bought by the Earl of Arundel from Queen Mary, and finished by him, as he said, for the love he bore to his old master, and "for the honour of this realme as a pearle thereof." Elizabeth bought it back from his son-in-law Lord Lumley. It was settled on Anne of Denmark; afterwards on Henrietta Maria; was occupied during the Commonwealth by General Lambert and by Colonel Pride who died there in 1658; and after the Restoration, it seems to have fallen into neglect. In the time of the Plague and also during the great fire the office of the exchequer was moved to Nonsuch. Evelyn supped there in 1666, and has left a description of it. In 1670 Charles II gave it to Barbara Villiers, Duchess of Cleveland, one of his mistresses, "another lady of pleasure and curse of our nation," as Evelyn says, who promptly dismantled it to pay her debts, sold the furniture, and cut up the parks into farms. Part of the building was still to be seen in 1757, but no trace of it now remains. It survives only in Hoefnagel's engraving (Plate IV).

The palace consisted of two courts, of which the inner was raised eight feet above the other and approached by steps. This was a very "faire and very curious structure

Nonsuch palace

Its destruction

The two courts

[1] Law, *op. cit.* vol. I. p. 161.

or building of two stories high, the lower storie whereof is of good and well-wrought freestone, and the higher of wood richly adorned and set forth and garnished with a variety of statues, pictures, and other antick formes of excellent art and workmanship, and of no small cost, all which building lying upon a square is covered with blue slate, and incloseth one faire and large court of one hundred and thirty and seaven foot broad, and one hundred and sixteen foot long, all paved with freestone, commonly called the inner court.".........The inner court had wooden battlements covered with lead, "adding a very great grace and special ornament to the whole building, and had large angle turrets at east and west five storeys high, of timber covered with lead, the chief ornament of the whole house[1]." (Plate IV.)

Italian plaster decora-tions

The Duke of Saxe Weimar[2] early in the 16th century describes the plaster figures. He says the " Labours of Hercules were set forth on the King's side, the Queen's side exhibiting all kinds of heathen stories with naked female figures."

Visit by Pepys

Pepys, in 1663, says: "we went through Nonsuch Park to the house, and viewed as much as we could of the outside, and looked through the great gates, and found a noble court, and altogether believe it to have been a very noble house, and a delicate park about it." It seems however already to have been suffering from neglect. In 1665, when the Exchequer was at Nonsuch on account of the Plague, Pepys was there again. He says[3] he walked up and down the house and park; "and a fine

---

[1] Report of the Parliamentary Commissioners in 1650, *Victoria County History of Surrey*, vol. III. p. 266, etc. Hoefnagel's print seems to show the outside of this second court.

[2] Cited, Blomfield, *Renaissance Architecture in England*, vol. II. p. 362.

[3] *Diary*, Sept. 21, 1665.

Plate III

PALATIVM REGIVM IN ANGLIÆ REGNO APPELLATVM NONCIVTZ,
Hoc est nusquam simile.

Effigiauit Georgius Hoefnaglius Anno 1582.

NONSUCH

place it hath heretofore been, and a fine prospect about the house. A great walk of an elme and a walnutt set after one another in order. And all the house on the outside filled with figures of stories, and good painting of Rubens' or Holbein's doing. I walked also into the ruined garden."

Evelyn in 1666 describes the "plaster statues and basse relievos of the inner court inserted 'twixt the timbers and punchions of the outside walles of the Court: which must needs have been the work of some celebrated *Italian.* I much admired," he continues, "how it had lasted so well and intire since the time of Henry VIII, exposed as they are to the aire, and pitty it is they are not taken out and preserved in some drie place; a gallery would become them. There are some mezzo rilievos as big as the life, the storie is of yᵉ Heathen Gods, emblems, compartments &c. The Palace consists of 2 courts, of which the first is of stone, castle-like, by yᵉ *Lo Lumlies* (of whom 'twas purchas'd) ye other of timber, a Gotiq fabric, but these walls incomparably beautified. I observed that the appearing timber punchions, entrelices, &c. were all so covered with scales of slate that it seemed carv'd in the wood and painted, yᵉ slate fastened on the timber in pretty figures, that has like a coate of armour preserved it from rotting." Pepys however says that "the posts and quarters in the walls are covered with lead and gilded[1]." "There stand in the garden," continues Evelyn, "2 handsome stone pyramids and the avenue planted with rows of faire elmes, but the rest of these goodly trees, both of this and Worcester Park adjoyning were felled by those destructive and avaricious rebells in the late warr, wᶜʰ defac'd one of the stateliest seates his Mᵗʸ had[2]."

Visit by Evelyn

The stucco figures

The garden and park

---

[1] Pepys, *Diary*, Sept. 21, 1665.   [2] Evelyn, *Diary*, Jan. 3, 1666.

Nonsuch
Palace

The defacement, however, as we have seen, was completed by one of his Majesty's mistresses.

If ·the rude representation of the house in Speed's *Theatre of the British Empire* mày be trusted the outside of the inner court as well as the inside was adorned with plaster figures apparently life size, both on the ground floor and the upper. Between them seems to be a mezzanine with cartouche work round the windows.

The
garden and
fountains

Of further adornments there was a fountain of white marble and bronze in the inner court; and in the Privie garden which surrounded the inner court on three sides, and was enclosed by the high wall shown in Hoefnagel's print, there was a marble fountain, placed between the marble pinnacles or pyramids of which Evelyn speaks. Round this were set six trees called "lilack trees, which trees beer no fruit, but only a very pleasant flower." They were novelties in England then.

Nonsuch Palace, of which Leland writes,

> Hanc quia non habeat similem laudare Britanni
> Saepe solent, *nullique parem* cognomine dicunt,

The
architect
unknown

seems to have deserved its name, not only for its singularity but also for its beauty. Camden says that "it is so magnificent, and withal so beautiful, as to arrive at the highest pitch of ostentation; and one would think that the whole art of architecture had been crowded into this single work. So many images to the life are upon the sides of it, so many wonders of workmanship as might even vie with the remains of Antiquity[1]." On the strength of a passage in Vasari it has been said that the architect was

Toto della
Nunziata

a Florentine, Toto della Nunziata. Toto was a pupil of Ridolfo Ghirlandajo, who had many young lads in his

---

[1] *Magna Britannia.* Particulars of Nonsuch were collected by the late Mr Kershaw, F.S.A., for an article in *Bygone Surrey*.

shop, whose emulation among themselves made them excellent artists. In particular Pierino del Vaga and Toto della Nunziata were inspired by mutual rivalry to achieve excellence. Many of his pupils were recommended by Ridolfo for employment in England, Germany, and Spain. Toto left Italy with some Florentine merchants for England, "where," says Vasari, "he has done all his works, and where he received the greatest recognition from the king, whom he served also in the matter of architecture and in particular made the principal palace[1]."

Anthony, or Toto della Nunziata, is mentioned in the privy purse accounts of 1530 where it appears that he and Bartholomewe or Luca Penni, painters of Florence, are engaged at the rate of £25 a year. In 1537 Toto was granted letters of naturalization and appointed sergeant painter to the king. He was employed by Henry in continuing the work at Hampton Court, and he painted six pictures for the king's Library, and four more for his closet[2].

But it is impossible to accept an Italian as the Architect of Nonsuch, supposing that to be the Palace referred to by Vasari. The building was Gothic, as Evelyn says, though "incomparably beautified." This beautification by plaster imagery was no doubt as Evelyn says by Italians, and in that Toto may have been employed, as well as in other decorative work both inside and outside, while the actual architecture would naturally be carried out by English designers. The fountains of marble and bronze would probably be the work of Italians. The text in Braun's *Urbium Principuarum mundi Theatrum quintum*,

---

[1] Vasari, *Vita di Dom° Puligo*, and do. *di Pierino del Vaga*.

[2] Walpole's *Anecdotes*, and Paper by Digby Wyatt, cited by Sir Reginald Blomfield, *Renaissance Architecture in England*, vol. I. p. 15.

Foreign artists as decorators

where Hoefnagel's engraving appears, says the king engaged at regal expense artists of various nations—Italian, French and Dutch, as well as natives, who showed their art in decorating this palace with statues within and without, equalling or excelling the Antiquities of Rome[1]. This does not seem to cover the architectural structure itself, but to refer to the decoration bestowed on it.

[1] Diversarum nationum praestantes opifices, architectos, sculptores, et statuarios, Italos, Gallos, Hollandos, et patriotas sumptu regio invitavit, qui mirabile artis suae experimentum in hac arce ediderunt, statuis eam intus et foris condecorarunt magnificis quae Romanas antiquitates partim apprime referunt partim superant. Quoted Blomfield, *op. cit.* vol. I. p. 17, who says it it very rare to find mention of a French artist during this period.

Plate IV

SUTTON PLACE

From *Country Life*

Plate V

SUTTON PLACE

From *Country Life*

CHAPTER III

THE EARLY RENAISSANCE (*continued*)

MANY examples of Early Renaissance work in England are, as we shall see, by well-known Italian artists, who came to us with an established reputation. But there is a good deal of decorative work in minor details of which it is difficult to say whether it was done by Italian craftsmen, or by Englishmen who had caught the new manner from Italians employed in their neighbourhood, and perhaps on the same building. The pendants of the roof at Hampton Court by Rydge (Figs. 7 and 8) are an example of Renaissance work done by an English *karver* in 1530, which but for the testimony of the accounts one would not hesitate to assign to an Italian. It is equally puzzling to know whether to assign the terra-cotta ornamentation of Sutton Place in Surrey to Italian workmen of inferior skill, or to Englishmen doing their best to work in the new manner.

SUTTON PLACE near Guildford was built between 1520 and 1530 by Sir Richard Weston[1] (Plate IV). Like the Marneys, Fitzwilliams, Seymours, Boleyns, and his friend William Lord Sandys, he was one of the king's creatures; a courtier who through thick and thin served his master and managed to retain his confidence to the last. He saw many of his colleagues sent to the block; his own son was accused and executed on a trumped up charge of intrigue

[1] Mr Frederic Harrison thinks the exact date of the building is between 1521 and 1527. *Annals of an old Manor House, Sutton Place, Guildford* p. 121.

with Anne Boleyn, but it made no difference in his faithful service to the royal murderer. He writes to Wolsey
that he owes all he has to his "Grace's goodness and
medyacian," though he is all the while in high favour with
the Cardinal's enemy Anne Boleyn, as he was afterwards
with her rival and successor Jane Seymour. In all this he
was no worse than the politicians of his day; he was only
a typical member of the new aristocracy; an instrument
of Royal aggrandizement—on which his own interest
depended.

The manor of Sutton was granted to Sir Richard
Weston by the king in 1521, and further grants were
made in 1530. The house of Sutton Place, is an early
example of the unfortified manor. There is not even a
moat, and the outer walls are as liberally supplied with
spacious windows as those facing the courtyard. It was
planned in the English fashion round a quadrangle 81 feet
square, and entered through a stately gateway tower with
angle turrets like the houses I have already described.
The material is red brick, with diapers of glazed black
headers and dressings of terra-cotta. The north wing with
the entrance tower was pulled down in 1782, but the rest
of Weston's building remains complete.

The plan (Fig. 9) is for the date remarkably symmetrical. The doors and windows on each side of the court
correspond, and there is a projecting oriel in the middle
of the east side opposite another in the middle of the west.
The great hall is opposite the entrance, and is now entered
by a door in the axial line of the court exactly opposite
the entrance gateway, instead of being as Dr Boorde
directs, not exactly opposite but yet somewhat "a base"
of it. On the opposite side of the hall facing south and
leading to the garden is another door on the same axial

line, which suggests that the bay containing these doors The Hall
was not originally part of the hall but was screened off and
formed the usual buttery passage. There is however no
evidence for this. Symmetry also dictated that the middle
part of the hall-block facing the entrance (Plate V) should

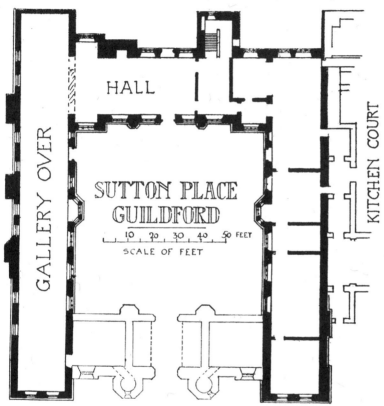

HALL

GALLERY OVER

SUTTON PLACE
GUILDFORD

10   20   30   40   50 FEET
SCALE OF FEET

KITCHEN COURT

Fig. 9.

be raised above the rest and be flanked by two semi- The centre
octagonal tourelles, though there is nothing inside to be piece
expressed by this difference ; and also that in the angles of
the court right and left there should be two similar projections, one for the hall-oriel, while the other has no special

The Hall
not dis-
tinguished purpose except to pair with it. Symmetrical arrangement also forbade the lofty windows usual in a hall which rises through two storeys, and directed that the tiers of windows of the two storeys in the rest of the building should not be interrupted, so that the hall is lighted by two tiers of

Fig. 10.

windows one above the other. There is consequently nothing in the outside elevation to tell one where the hall is, or whether there is any hall at all.

Details
Gothic

The details of the architecture throughout are purely English in the late Gothic style. The doors have four-

centred arches under a square head with traceried spandrils, the windows are mullioned and square headed, with
trefoiled and cinquefoiled cusped lights. The mouldings
round the windows and doors are all purely Gothic (Fig. 10)
and quatrefoils mixed with other forms appear in the
parapets. The gable ends of the east and west wings are
crow-stepped, an unusual feature in England at this
period and possibly adopted here to save stone copings,
for there is hardly any stone whatever in the building.

Fig. 11.

Stone as we have seen in buildings already described had
to be economized in districts where it could only be
brought by land, on account of the difficulty and expense
of transport; and the only building stone in that part of
Surrey is chalk, not a durable material, though for want
of a better the dressings and window traceries of the
churches were made of it from the 12th to the 15th centuries. It may have been partly for this reason that
Sir Richard Weston decided to use terra-cotta instead of
stone for his architectural details. All the doorways,

Terra-cotta dressings

windows and parapets are in this material, though as will be seen by the details (Fig. 10) they are all profiled in the regular Gothic style. So far as this goes the whole work

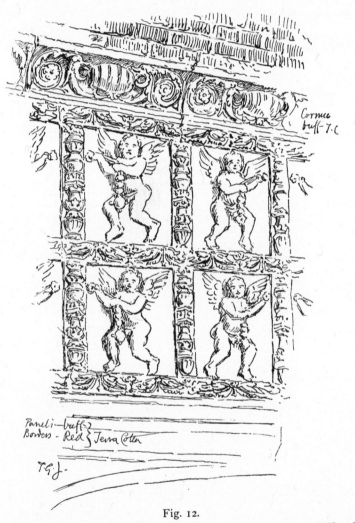

Fig. 12.

The style English

is purely English, but with the decoration a difficulty arises. The octagonal turrets are cased with terra-cotta bricks about $11'' \times 9\frac{1}{2}''$, on which are worked Sir Richard's

initials R. W. alternately with the punning device of a
tun, and with angle bricks bearing a trefoil between
bunches of grapes (Fig. 11). This again might be an
English design ; but what are we to say of the little winged Italian
children that run right and left in panels over the doors details
and elsewhere, divided by candelabra and borders with

Fig. 13.

the classic husk ; or of the dolphins and scrolls that
alternate with the tun in the cornice above (Fig. 12); or
of the ornament laid along the hollow mouldings of the
windows, which are unlike anything known to the British
carver or modeller (Fig. 13) ? All this is either Italian
work or work imitative of Italian design, and thoroughly
un-English.

It is natural to enquire to what these peculiarities are due, who was the architect, and how did the Italian element come in? Mr Harrison suggests that "the general artistic superintendence and finer ornamental work may have been due to Trevisano" and the same suggestion has been made with reference to Layer Marney, where the Italian influence is still more remarkable and Girolamo Trevisano the execution is superior. This artist, Girolamo da Trevigi, was a painter of whom Vasari says he was a pleasant colourist though not very great in design, and that he imitated the style of Raffaelle. He was employed largely in his own city and at Venice and Bologna, but thinking himself ill used in a competition, in which he was unsuccessful, he came to England, where he was introduced by his friends to Henry VIII. The king engaged him not as a painter but as an engineer; made him director not the Architect of his buildings with a salary of 400 scudi a year, and gave him a house. He was cut in two by a cannon-ball in the 36th year of his age[1] at the siege of Boulogne in 1544 where he was directing the artillery. He would therefore have been born in 1508 and would have been only 16 at the date of Henry Lord Marney's death, and not much older when Sir Richard Weston was building his house; and this disposes of his connexion with either of these buildings ; for though Vasari does not say when he came to England, the long list of his works in Italy shows that it must have been late in his short-lived career. But independently of dates the Italianizing ornament at Sutton Place cannot be attributed to an artist of much repute, for it must be admitted that it does not reach

[1] Onde in un medesimo tempo la vita e gli honori del mondo, insieme con le grandezze sue rimasero estinte, essendo egli nell' età d' anni 36 l' anno MDXLIV. Vasari, *Vite*, etc.

a high Italian standard. The little devices that lie in the hollow of the mullions and jambs are unmeaning and not interesting, and the little cherubs or amorini, though quaint and delightfully amusing in their way, would have shocked Civitale, and would have been disowned by Trevisano or Benedetto da Rovezzano who were working a little later in England. If not by Englishmen trying their hands at Italian ornament, they may have been done by Italian artists of a lower grade than the men whose names we know. These greater men would bring with them operatives to work under them. We read for instance of John de Manns, or Demans, or Demyans, as the English called Giovanni da Majano, and *his company*; who were no doubt skilled Italians capable of undertaking work on their own account, though not great artists: and some of these lesser men may have found their way to Sutton and done these things for Sir Richard Weston. They must have taught the Englishmen how to make terra-cotta, which is an Italian and especially a Lombard art, practised in the great plain of the Po where stone is as scarce as it is in Surrey. In return the English must have been responsible for profiling the English mouldings in the new material, for in the sections of jamb and arch there is no trace whatever of any but English design, which no Italian could have imagined.

The best parts of the terra-cotta work are the cornice with the tuns between dolphin-scroll-work, and the horizontal bands with husks and vases, neither of which could, I think, have been devised by an Englishman at that time (Fig. 14, p. 46).

The terra-cotta is of two colours; generally buff, but the borders round the panels with the children are red. Compared with the contemporary terra-cotta designs at

Layer Marney that at Sutton shows less skill in execution, and less knowledge of Renaissance work, the Italian ornament being applied to work purely English.

Fig. 14.

Symmetry
at Sutton
Place   As to the symmetry of the plan, which is insisted upon even at the expense of convenience, I can only suppose it due to a fancy of Sir Richard's. Symmetry is more observed in Italy, but we do not hear of his having been in that country, and though he was in France the contemporary chateaux of Francis I, and others which he may have seen, are not remarkable for symmetrical planning.

The Vyne   At the same time that Sir Richard Weston was building his house near Guildford, his friend and fellow-courtier William Lord Sandys was engaged in making THE VYNE near Basingstoke, which he found "no very great or sumptuous Manor House," into one of the principal seats in Hampshire. It had belonged to the Sandys, or their relatives the Brocas family since the time of Richard II, and the Sandys held it till the Commonwealth when it was bought by Sir Chaloner Chute, Speaker of Richard Cromwell's Parliament, in whose family it has since remained. The new owner altered it a good deal in 1654 Modernized by
Webb when he employed Webb, Inigo Jones's kinsman and pupil, to modernize it by building a "Grecian" portico at the back or garden side, and by cutting the old windows square and fitting them with sashes at 16 shillings apiece.

This of course has robbed the house of much of its antiquity outside[1].

John Chute who succeeded in 1754, and died in 1776, the friend of Gray and Walpole, made further alterations, and added the present charmingly picturesque staircase, and the tomb chamber adjoining the chapel with the monument of Speaker Chaloner Chute by Bankes.

The history of William Lord Sandys is very like that of Sir Richard Weston. Like him he took part in the political trials or rather the judicial murders of the day, for they were nothing else[2]. He sat as one of the judges appointed to find poor Anne Boleyn guilty. He served with Weston in France in 1523 under Charles Brandon, Duke of Suffolk, where he distinguished himself and won his peerage. He was made a Knight of the Garter in 1518 like Henry Lord Marney, and Lord Chamberlain in 1526. He died in 1540, and was buried in the pretty aisle he had added to the Chapel of the Holy Ghost, which one sees from the railway at Basingstoke.

Lord Sandys

The Vyne which is said to have been begun about 1509 is an unfortified house, now consisting of an E-shaped block with an extension eastwards containing the chapel.

The Vyne unfortified

---

[1] For taking down the old windows, and setting up the

new, cut into square heads	£0 16s. 0d. each
For material, workmanship and setting of the pillar (? *and*) capitals of the Portico in Burford stone ...	£13 0s. 0d. each
For the pillar bases in Portland stone	£5 0s. 0d. each
For the pilaster bases	£4 0s. 0d. each
For the Frontispiece over the Portico with Chaloner Chute's arms	£3 0s. 0d.

A History of the Vyne in Hampshire, p. 138, by Chaloner W. Chute, of the Vyne.

[2]   Can you think, Lords,
That any Englishman dare give me counsel?
Or be a known friend, 'gainst his Highness' pleasure?
                                        King Henry VIII, Act III. sc. i.

The base
court

There was however formerly a "basse court" behind, built by Lord Sandys, which was pulled down by Chaloner Chute. It contained among other rooms, two long dormitories for the yeomen with twelve beds in each, a schoolmaster's chamber and an armoury. There is a certain symmetry both in the front and the back, but the plan is

Unusual
plan

unusual, divided lengthways by massive walls, and the hall, which is generally the principal feature on the ground floor is not defined (Fig. 15).

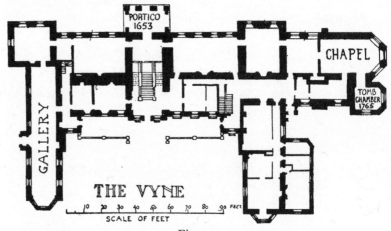

Fig. 15.

The
Chapel

Horace Walpole says, "at the Vyne is the most heavenly chapel in the world." It remains very much unaltered as Lord Sandys built it. There is an apse of three sides, with three Perpendicular windows, but the high-pitched roof does not cover the apse and is stopped on the chord with a gable and bargeboard. Like the rest of the house the chapel is built of red brick with chequers of grey headers and stone dressings. The stalls and panelling are good, and a grotesque poppy head, where the turnover is represented by acrobatic figures, intertwined and curved backwards, reminds one of a capital in the cloister at Cefalù in Sicily consisting of acrobats looking through their legs, which are turned up over their shoulders. The general design of the woodwork is in late Gothic style but there are scrolls of foliage and figures in the cornice of a Renaissance character, though more Flemish than Italian. Elsewhere a more Italian character appears in the decoration.

The apse windows are filled with excellent painted glass of which the upper part at all events seems to be foreign, and is said to have been brought by Lord Sandys from France.

The Vyne has no terra-cotta dressings, and indeed the use of that material in England is to be found chiefly in the east and south east. Torrigiano, the Florentine sculptor, who was in England in 1511 or possibly a little earlier, was perhaps the first to introduce it into this country. He was famous for his skill in working it. Michel-Angelo, we are told, made his first essay in marble, inspired by what he saw Torrigiano doing in clay[1]. Francesco d'Olanda, writing of celebrated sculptors who were his contemporaries, speaks of *Maestro Pietro Torrigiano, modellatore di terra*, and says he made a portrait in clay of the Empress (of Portugal[2]). His effigy in terra-cotta of Dr Young, formerly in the Rolls Chapel, is well known; and the altar he designed in Henry VII's chapel had a figure of a dead Christ below it, and on the canopy four angels with instruments of the passion, all of "erthe baked in an oven." The reredos of the same altar was modelled in terra-cotta, with the Resurrection on one side and the

---

[1] See Part I. *Italy*, p. 22.

[2] *Archaeological Journal*, 1894, p. 152. Article on *The work of Florentine Sculptors in England*, by Alfred Higgins, F.S.A.

Nativity of Christ on the other, framed in marble and bronze. At East Barsham House in Norfolk and Great Snoring Rectory near it, there is terra-cotta work; that at East Barsham is studded with little plaques with well modelled human heads that have rather a Flemish look. At Cressingham Manor House in Norfolk the outer walls are panelled with terra-cotta work, in which the windows with simple Gothic tracery are also constructed. The roundels and heraldic panels at Hampton Court have been described already; similar roundels in terra-cotta were in Holbein's gate of Whitehall palace which has disappeared; and terra-cotta was used in tombs at Arundel and Box-

grove in Sussex. All these buildings, like Sutton Place, it will be observed, are in districts where there was no local freestone available, and where brick was the usual building material. Its use is connected with the presence of Italian workmen in England, and when after the death of Henry VIII the Italians went home, the use of terra-cotta in England disappeared with them.

CHAPTER IV

TOMBS OF THE KINGS AND CARDINAL WOLSEY

THE tomb of Henry VII, now in the chapel of which he laid the foundation at Westminster in 1503, and which in 1508–9 was ready for glazing and painting according to the provision made in his will, was originally intended to be placed in the Lady Chapel or Tomb-house at Windsor. Payments had been made in 1501–2 to "Master Esterfelde on account of the Kinge's Toumbe at Windsor," and it would seem that the bronze screen, or "grate in the manner of a closure," that surrounds the tomb was partly done. In 1502–3 however Master Esterfelde received £68. 3s. 2d. for conveying the whole to Westminster, a sum equal to £700 of our money, which implies a good deal of work partly or wholly completed[1].

Henry VII's tomb at Windsor

removed to Westminster

The first design for the tomb was made by Guido Mazzoni of Modena, known as Paganino, or in England as Master Pageny. He was the author of a life-size group in terra-cotta of the Deposition from the cross in the church of Monte Oliveto at Naples, which was so much admired by Charles VIII that he dubbed the sculptor knight, and brought him back with him to France in 1495, on his return from that mischievous Italian expedition. Guido made the monument of Charles VIII in marble and bronze, and though nothing remains of his work for Henry VII his design seems to have been similar to that for Charles at S. Denis. There were to be bronze figures of the king and queen within the tomb, and on the top a kneeling

First design by Paganino

[1] For the full history of these tombs, see Mr Higgins's article above cited.

4—2

Tomb for
Henry VII

figure of the king with four of his lords, and there were to be twelve small images of virtues round about the tomb. For making "patrones" in timber from which these nineteen figures were to be cast in bronze competitive estimates were obtained from "*Lawrence Ymber, karver,*" and Drawsword, Sheriff of York. Imber's price was £64 and Drawsword's £36[1]. Drawsword was a well-known "imager" of that day, and at one time member of Parliament and Mayor of his native city. For Charles VIII's virtues, Henry VII by his will substituted his ten *avouries* or favourite saints, S. Michael, the two SS. John, S. George, S. Anthony, S. Vincent, S. Anne, S. Edward, S. Mary Magdalene and S. Barbara.

First
design
rejected

Henry VIII, however, disliked the design, and it was not carried out.

Arrival of
Torrigiano

In 1511, if not sooner, the Florentine Pietro Torrigiano came to England in the company of some merchants, his countrymen. He had found it prudent to leave Florence after the blow by which he disfigured Michel-Angelo for life, and after serving for some time as a soldier, he had returned to his art of sculpture. In 1511 he contracted for £400 to make the tomb in Westminster Abbey of the Lady Margaret Beaufort, mother of Henry VII. The agreement is drawn between Fisher, Bishop of Rochester and seven others, executors of the lady's will, among whom was

Contract
for the
tomb of
Lady
Margaret

Henry Marney Knight, and "Petir Thoryson of fflorence graver." Torrigiano "bargayneth with the said Executours to make or cause to be made at his owne propre cost and charge, wele, clenly, and sufficiently and workemanly a Tabernacle of copper with an ymage lying in the same Tabernacle, and a best called an yas (? yale) lying at the fote of the same...and furthermore...he bindeth hym by

[1] Lethaby, *Westminster Abbey and the King's Craftsmen*, p. 234.

these presents to worke or do to be made a Tombe otherwise called the case of a Tombe of good clene and hable towche stone with all such workmanship in the same as shalbe according to patrone drawen, and kerven in Tymbre and signed with thand and sealed with the seale of the said Petir[1]."

The image of Lady Margaret, Countess of Richmond, lies on an altar tomb of black marble or touch-stone in the south aisle of her son's chapel. The sides and ends of the tomb are decorated with escutcheons surmounted by crowns or coronets, within wreaths of foliage, divided by pilasters. All this is obviously Italian work, except the heraldry on the shields which is inserted on thin bronze plates, and which Mr Higgins therefore suggests were done independently by English workmen. The splendid modelling of the figure, and of the hands, withered by old age, is of course well known to all students and lovers of art, and is worthy of the best Florentine traditions. The tabernacle within which the lady lies, on the other hand, cannot possibly be the work of an Italian of the 16th century, for it is in the regular Gothic style of the Tudor period, and must be by English workmen acting probably for Torrigiano under the direction of Bolton, Prior of S. Bartholomew's in Smithfield, who was entrusted with the supervision of Master Petir Torrysany. *Lady Margaret's tomb*

The iron grille which has lately been recovered and replaced round the tomb was made by Cornelyus Symondson, of the parish of S. Clement Danes for £22. It was given by S. John's College in memory of their Foundress. *The grille*

---

[1] The documents relating to the tomb of Lady Margaret have come to light in the Muniment room of S. John's College, one of her two foundations at Cambridge, v. paper by the Master of S. John's College in *Archaeologia*, vol. LXVI. 1914–15, p. 365.

One item in the accounts for my Lady's tomb must be mentioned before we leave the subject :

> Item paide the xxvijth day of December, the seide iiij yere to M. Erasmus for the ephitaff aboute my ladies tombe by my lordes commaundment.   20s. 0d.[1]

Torrigi-
ano's con-
tract for
Henry
VII's
tomb
The admiration excited by this masterpiece of Petir Torrysany led to his engagement in the following year to make the tomb of Henry VII and his queen Elizabeth of York. On Oct. 26, 1512, Torrigiano contracts with the executors of the late king "to make and worke, or do to be made and wrought well, surely, clenly and workmanly, curiously and substancyally for the sum of £1500 sterling a tombe or sepulture of whit marbill and of black touche-stone wᵗ ymags, figures, beasts, and other things of coppure gilt...togedir wᵗ other dyv'se ymags, epitaphies and other things." The tomb was finished in January 1518–9. On the sides are wreaths carved in touch-stone like those on the Countess of Richmond's tomb, but instead of heraldry they enclose medallions of bronze of the king's ten *avouries,* with the addition of two more, S. Christopher and the Virgin and child. They are grouped in pairs, two figures to each medallion. Four angels sit at the corners of the upper part, and the figures of the king and queen in gilded bronze are not inferior to that of the royal Lady in the adjoining aisle. As in her tomb the heraldry here also appears to be by English hands, as was observed by Sir W. St J. Hope and Mr Higgins (Plate VI). The bronze screen that encloses the tomb is Gothic, and no doubt of native work, and Professor Lethaby suggests that the little figures in the niches, of which unfortunately several are missing, may be by Laurence Imber[2].

[1] *Documents at S. John's College*, in *Archaeologia, op. cit.* p. 370, where there is a good illustration of the tomb.   [2] *op. cit.* p. 235.

Plate VI

WESTMINSTER ABBEY—TOMB OF HENRY VII

While the tomb was in progress Torrigiano contracted in 1516–7 to make the altar at its west end. Little progress had been made with it in 1518, when he wrote to Wolsey[1] that he must go to Florence for matters connected with the completion of the work, and that he had only waited in order to settle about some other work promised him by the king, apparently a tomb for Henry VIII and Queen Katharine which was then projected. Losing patience, a quality for which he was not remarkable, Torrigiano went to Florence without leave in 1519, and there was a great to do to get him back. The Florentine Consul wrote to the Signory to beg them to send him to England, as the good faith of the Florentine colony in London was pledged, as well as that of his sureties, for the due performance of his engagements. He was sent back or returned of his own accord at the end of the year, bringing with him Antonio di Lorenzo a sculptor, and Toto della Nunziata the painter of whom we have heard already, though he had failed, as we know from Benvenuto Cellini, to induce that equally truculent genius to come with him[2].

His altar in Henry VII's chapel was destroyed by the Puritans in 1643, but from fragments that were collected and put together by Dean Stanley, and from old engravings and descriptions the design can be recovered. The altar table was of touch-stone resting on marble piers at the angles and bronze balusters in front, and underneath was a "bakyn image of erthe coloured of Christ dede." At the back of the altar was a reredos or *dosel* of terra-cotta framed in bronze, with a relief of the Resurrection facing

---

[1] The letter is in Latin. It is given in full by Mr Higgins, *op. cit.* Appendix I.

[2] Benvenuto says Torrigiano told him how he had broken Michel-Angelo's nose, upon which Benvenuto, who idolized Michel-Angelo, says, "so far from wishing to go with him to England, *non potevo patire di vederlo.*" *Vita*, Lib. I.

The altar, Henry VII's chapel

west, and another of the Nativity on the back facing east. Four bronze columns, raised on elaborately modelled pedestals carried a canopy with an elaborate entablature of architrave frieze and cornice all round it, perhaps of gilt bronze, on which stood the royal arms with lion and griffin supporters, and with two kneeling angels in terra-cotta, one holding a cross, and the other a column surmounted by a cock. This superstructure proved too heavy for the bronze supports, and Rovezzano replaced them afterwards by stronger[1]. The details that are preserved are beautiful, but the general design, if we may judge by Sandford's print of it, does not much commend itself.

Monument of Dr Young

The fine terra-cotta effigy of Dr Young, a friend of Erasmus, and Master of the Rolls, is now in the new Record Office whither it was removed when the Rolls chapel was destroyed. It was made by Torrigiano during the progress of the tomb of Henry VII.

Henry VIII's tomb in abeyance

The projected tomb of Henry VIII and Queen Katharine came to nothing, though in 1518–9 Torrigiano had contracted to make it for £2000 of white marble and touch-stone like Henry VII's tomb, but "more grettir by the iiij[th] parte." It was not even settled where it was to be, though the king at one time thought of building another chapel for it, to match or eclipse that of his father.

Cardinal Wolsey's tomb

This royal tomb remaining in abeyance, Wolsey designed a tomb for himself which would have been scarcely less magnificent. It was to be in the Eastern or Lady Chapel of S. George's at Windsor where it had first been

---

[1] A print of this altar in Sandford's *Genealogical History of the Kings of England* is reproduced in Mr Higgins's article, and in Dean Stanley's *Memorials of Westminster Abbey*, p. 513.

proposed to place the monument of Henry VII. Of Wolsey's tomb, however, Lord Herbert of Cherbury says "the design was so glorious that it exceeded far that of Henry the Seventh." The artist employed was another Florentine, Benedetto da Rovezzano, known to the English as Rovessanne or Rovesham. Torrigiano had gone to Spain, leaving England probably when the scheme for the king's tomb failed. His tragic end in the dungeons of the Inquisition is well known.

Benedetto da Rovezzano was a year older than Michel-Angelo, and had done important works in Florence, of which little remains, for the tomb of S. Gualberto of Vallombrosa, on which he was engaged ten years, was unfortunately destroyed during the siege of Florence in 1530 before it was erected. Lastly, says Vasari, " he went to England in the service of the king, for whom he did many works in marble and bronze, and in particular his sepulchre, from which works he gained enough to live comfortably the rest of his life. Wherefore having returned to Florence, after finishing some little things the dizziness (*vertigini*) which even in England had begun to injure his eyes, and other impediments caused thereby as they say from standing too much about the fire when founding his metals, or for some other reason, in a little while deprived him of all the light of his eyes, so that his work came to an end about 1550 and his life a few years later. Benedetto bore his blindness with Christian patience, thanking God that he had means to live with credit[1]."

Wolsey's tomb was never finished ; the work came to an end at his fall, and the best account of it is the inventory of the several parts given by Rovezzano when the king took possession of what had been done. The effigy of the

Marginal notes:
Benedetto da Rovezzano

Rovezzano's blindness and departure

The tomb never finished

[1] Vasari, *Vita di Benedetto da Rovezzano.*

Wolsey's
tomb

Cardinal in bronze gilt and burnished was finished : as were also four great pillars of bronze 9 feet high curiously graven, and four angels to stand upon them with candlesticks, and four naked boys with escutcheons of arms ; also the tomb of touch-stone, and various bronze plaques for epitaphs, and several other ornaments. There were "gryphons" and the Cardinal's hat with "xij buttons and certen strings of copper all gilt and burnished," and twelve little saints a foot long, and several decorative emblems. For the work done Rovezzano had received payment of £956. 5s. 0d., taking the value of the ducat at 4s. 6d., equal to more than £10,000 of our money. The gilding was a very expensive item ; for the whole tomb it would have cost £800, of which half had been done.

Wolsey's
tomb
taken by
the king
for himself

All this was seized by Henry on Wolsey's fall, and designed to be used for his own monument of which the intention was now revived. Wolsey begged, through Cromwell, for his effigy and such parts of the tomb as the king would graciously allow him that he might put them in his cathedral at York, but he begged in vain[1].

The tomb
never
finished

Henry's tomb shared the fate of Wolsey's : for it was never finished. Benedetto, who had worked on the tomb for Wolsey from 1524 to 1529, continued for six years more to work on it for the king ; after which the scheme was dropped again, owing perhaps to Rovezzano's failing sight and his return to Florence. The king died in 1547 leaving instructions for the completion of his tomb. Edward VI by will repeated this direction, but the suc-

---

[1] Mr Higgins, *op. cit.* p. 163, where a full detailed account is given of the history of these tombs. See also the documents in his Appendices. In his inventory of work done for Wolsey, Benedetto mentions six terra-cotta figures for the Cardinal's College at Oxford, of which nothing more is known. Mr Higgins suggests they may have been modelled, but not fired, when the Cardinal's fall interrupted the work.

ceeding disturbances prevented anything further being done at that time.

Henry's tomb was to be much finer even than Wolsey's. Instead of four great columns 9 feet high bearing angels 4½ feet high there were to be ten, four on a side and one more at each end, and between them were lofty candelabra. Wolsey's sarcophagus and base were raised on a podium, and the whole structure, which measured 26 feet by 13 feet, was to be enclosed by a bronze screen 4½ feet high. A good deal of this seems actually to have been made and put up in the chapel before the work was suspended. Queen Mary thought of finishing it, but remembered her father had died a schismatic. Elizabeth obtained from Burghley an account of what was still wanting towards completion but nothing more was done by her. Charles I seems to have intended it for his sepulture, but that of course came to nothing. The metal work was stripped and sold during the Civil Wars, and the last vestige of the structure was destroyed by the construction of the royal vaults in 1811. The sarcophagus intended first for the Cardinal and afterwards for the King now marks the resting-place of Nelson in S. Paul's Cathedral and four of the great bronze candelabra 9 feet high now stand in front of the high altar of the Church of S. Bavon at Ghent[1]. (Fig. 16, p. 60.)

Rovezzano's design, which Vasari tells us was preferred to a beautiful model by Baccio Bandinelli, was magnificently conceived. The effect of the lofty catafalque of black marble and white, carrying the royal effigy in gilt bronze, set within an avenue of bronze pillars 9 feet high carrying angelic figures, and alternating with exquisitely

Marginal notes: Rovezzano's design for Henry VIII's tomb — left incomplete — Its final disappearance — Beauty of the design

[1] Mr Higgins, with the cooperation of Mr Somers Clark, has ingeniously reconstructed both Wolsey's and Henry's tomb in his plates VI and VIII, *op. cit.* pp. 162, 190. There is a model of the candelabrum at S. Kensington (Fig. 16), and it has been reproduced at the choir of S. Paul's in bronze.

wrought candelabra (Fig. 16) would have been superb.
The nearest approach to its magnificence would have been
the tomb of Maximilian at
Innsbruck, surrounded by
ranks of heroes and paladins
in bronze; but there the
figures and the tomb are not
combined in a consistent
architectural design. The
tomb is low, and the figures
stand detached on the floor
at a distance from it. In
Rovezzano's conception we
see the masterly Florentine
touch, and had it been fully
realized there would have
been nothing to compare
worthily with it in any royal
monument in Christendom.

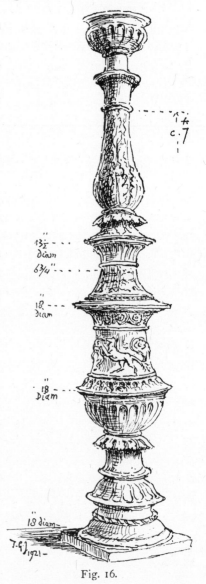

End of the
Italian
period
    With these splendid fail-
ures we reach the end of the
part played by Italians in
the history of the Renaissance in England. It ceased
with the reign of Henry
VIII. Its immediate influence was confined princi-
pally to the Capital, the
home counties, and East
Anglia, and even there it
influenced decorative details
rather than the general archi-

Fig. 16.

tecture, on which it had little direct effect. In every instance which we have reviewed English tradition asserted itself. Layer Marney has terra-cotta windows and battlements of Italian work, but they adorn the typical turretted gatehouse of an English mansion, and the mullioned lights of Gothic architecture. At Sutton Place every architectural feature, every moulding, every window, and every doorway is of pure Tudor Gothic, though Italianizing cherubs frisk in panels over the openings. At Lady Salisbury's chantry in Christchurch Priory the architecture is Gothic with traceried Perpendicular windows, fan-groining and crock-etted niches, though Italian carvers have been allowed to cut their graceful arabesques on the friezes and shafts outside. Even in the tombs, where the sculptor had a freer hand, he had to respect the national tradition. The free-standing altar tomb, which was the conventional English form, is not usual in Italy, but the tombs by Italians at Layer Marney, though they bear Renaissance ornament, conform to the regular English type. The canopy over Henry Lord Marney is an English not an Italian device; it resembles the testers over the tombs of the Black Prince and Henry IV at Canterbury, or those that surround the Confessor's chapel at Westminster; a conception carried out more completely and sumptuously in the chantries at Winchester, Bath, and Christchurch. English tradition asserts itself even in the royal tombs by Torrigiano at Westminster. Lady Margaret lies on a free-standing altar tomb of the usual form, though as at Layer Marney the sculptured sides are in the style of the Re-naissance, and the bronze tabernacle within which she lies is purely Gothic. The bronze screen of Henry VII's tomb is by native hands, with no trace of foreign art, but the Renaissance tomb inside is an altar tomb like that of the

Italian influence confined to decoration

Architec-ture still Gothic

king's mother in the adjoining aisle, though on a larger
scale; and in the heraldry at the ends English sculptors
seem to have had a hand, though they followed the lead
given them by the Italian master.

But the Italians had sown the seed from which the
Renaissance gradually sprang up, and in time affected
English architecture as it had that of France.   Classic
details gradually crept into the decoration of Gothic structures while the structure itself remained Gothic; as in
Bishop Gardiner's chantry at Winchester, where Perpendicular windows are surmounted by a Doric frieze with
triglyphs and ox-heads. Bishop Fox's chantry also has
Renaissance details: his arms are enclosed in a wreath
very unlike the Gothic character of the rest of the structure.
The mortuary chests which he placed on the side screens
of the choir are of Italian work decorated with colour on
gesso, and the stone base on which they rest is carved
with Italian arabesque. To him also may be attributed
the beautiful fragments of screens, now in the church of
the Hospital of S. Cross, which it is said were once in the
destroyed parish church of S. Faith (Plate VII). With their
heads of Roman emperors within a wreath, enclosed in a
Gothic cusp and surrounded by dolphins and classic scrolls,
they show a curious medley of styles. From these be-
ginnings the change gradually mounted to the architecture
itself. Henry VIII's second seal in 1532 was Gothic, like
the Hall he was then building at Hampton Court; his
third seal in 1542 is in the Renaissance style, by which,
in a figure, we may say the stamp of authority was affixed
to the coming change.

Plate VII

T. G. J.

S. CROSS—WINCHESTER

CHAPTER V

THE MIDDLE RENAISSANCE

DURING the rest of Henry VIII's reign the Renais- Slow pro-gress of the Re-naissance sance made little advance. The general character of the architecture remained Gothic, and it was only in minor decorative details that any signs of the new art appeared. At Ford Abbey, which dates from 1525–6, there are Italian ornaments in the frieze over the windows, and at Hengrave Hall, built at the same time as Ford Abbey, there is something of the same kind under the oriel. But the general design is Gothic in these buildings as it is at Cowdray, though the new style shows itself in the oriel vault, and cusping has disappeared from the heads of the lights. This however had happened already in many of the later Perpendicular churches, as at Bath Abbey, where the arched heads of the lights are alternately cusped and uncusped, and in Hatfield Church in Yorkshire and other places where cusping is omitted altogether. The next stage was to omit the arched head, and in the succeeding period the lights finish square at the top.

The Renaissance followed very much the same course The Re-naissance in France in France. The expedition of Charles VIII in 1494, the beginning of the disastrous interference of the foreigner in Italian politics, opened the eyes of the French nobility to the splendours of Italian art, and the superior refine-ment of Italian life. Charles shipped off a cargo of treasures of art, and followed it by a colony of twenty-two Italian Colonies of Italian workmen in France craftsmen whom he settled at Amboise. Other colonies were afterwards planted at Tours and Blois. As in

England, so in France it was only in decorative details at first, and for a considerable time, that Italian influence was felt, while the architecture remained Gothic. Like Henry VIII, though a little later, Francis I invited distinguished Italian artists to work for him. Henry had failed to induce Raffaelle and Titian to come to England, and though

Leonardo da Vinci was persuaded by Francis to come to France in 1516, he was old, his hand was partly paralysed, and he died in 1519; so that his coming had little or no effect on French architecture. It was not till 1530 and

1531 that Il Rosso and Primaticcio were engaged on the Chateau of Fontainebleau. But in spite of these Italian masters the work of the early French Renaissance has very little resemblance to that of Italy : less indeed than

Contrast
of Renais-
sance in
France
and
England
the contemporary work in England. In France the Renaissance inherited and exaggerated the lofty roofs and the enriched dormer windows of the Flamboyant style, such as those in the Palais de Justice at Rouen, which were translated into the semi-classic features of Chambord and Blois. In England on the contrary the new style followed the more restrained spirit of the Perpendicular period, when the high-pitched roofs of the decorated styles had sunk to the low-pitched or flat roofs of the 15th century, which were barely seen above the parapet; and in some of the palaces of the Early Renaissance as at Longleat and Burghley the roof disappears altogether from the outside view.

Henry VIII, with his love of splendour and display, and his extravagance in building, in furniture, and in entertainments, had exhausted the wealth which he inherited from his penurious father, and he left a legacy of debt to his successor. The reigns of Edward VI and Mary were brief and troublous, and when under the more settled

government of Elizabeth there was time to attend to the Architectural activity under Elizabeth chiefly secular
arts, architecture passed into a new phase. Ecclesiastical
architecture, which during the Middle Ages had almost
occupied the whole field of the Art, had now come to a
stand-still with the Reformation. Churches were no longer
built from motives of devotion apart from the need of
accommodation, and as the country was furnished super-
abundantly with houses of prayer, it would have been
superfluous to build more. The architecture of this and
the following reign therefore is almost entirely secular.
In secular architecture however extraordinary activity
prevailed. Noble vied with noble in the splendour and Palaces of the nobles
scale of their palaces, and rich traders housed themselves
with no less magnificence, and possibly even more comfort
than their superiors in rank. Planned to house the vast
family of retainers with which the nobles of those days
surrounded themselves, many of these mansions covered
several acres of ground with buildings far beyond any
modern requirements. The great house of Audley End
is said to occupy but a third or fourth part of its original
extent. On a smaller scale manor houses of the squires Manor houses throughout England
and wealthy yeomen sprang up all over the country,
testifying to the prosperity of the time. They were built
substantially of stone or brick, or of half-timbering where
oak forests supplied material more readily than the quarry;
and there is scarcely a village in the country districts
which cannot show some homestead of Elizabethan or
Jacobean times to delight us with its quaint simplicity,
and its modest beauty.

The Italian artists of Henry VIII's time had disap- Disappearance of Italians
peared probably for lack of employment, but Italy was
still regarded for a time as the fount of architecture. In
1550 John Shute, "Paynter and Archytecte" as he calls John Shute

John
Shute

himself was sent by the Duke of Northumberland to Italy "ther to cōfer wᵗ the doiges of yᵉ skilful Maisters in architectur and also to view such aūcīēt Monumētes hereof as are yet extant[1]." He published a book in 1563 with illustrations of the orders, and died the same year without so far as is known having done any building. But after the accession of Elizabeth and the rise of Protestantism, in-

Rupture
with
Catholic
powers

tercourse with Italy was impeded. The Queen was excommunicated in 1571 by Pius V, and again by Sixtus V who blessed the Armada in 1588 and fulminated a harmless Interdict against the kingdom. The Popes tried to prevent all intercourse between England and the Catholic countries, and Venice for a time withdrew her ambassador. These impediments naturally diverted English attention to the Low Countries, then in the throes of their conflict with the bigotry of Philip II, and the brutalities of Alva.

Attach-
ment to
the Ne-
therlands

They looked to Elizabeth as the champion of the Reformed Religion. Refugees from Flanders and Holland flocked into England, bringing many useful trades new to this country, as well as artizans of superior skill. They were

Immigra-
tion of
Dutch and
Flemings

settled by license in various towns especially in East Anglia and Kent; there were master workmen in cloth and fishers who revived industry at Sandwich; Norwich received 4000 Dutch refugees, and many more were settled about the county. Maidstone begged for foreign settlers to be sent there; lace workers were established at Honiton; and in time the immigration reached such proportions that it provoked discontent and riots, and had to be checked by authority.

These strangers brought with them traditions of the architecture in their old home which introduced a new

---

[1] Cited, Gotch, *op. cit.* vol. I. p. xix. Only two copies of the book are known to exist.

element into the English Renaissance. In the sister art Its effect on English art
of painting indeed artists from the Netherlands had come
even in Henry VIII's time: Lucas Herenbout of Ghent,
with his brother Gerard settled here as painters, with
their sister Susanna, a miniaturist[1]. Many pictures in
this country attributed to Holbein are supposed to be by
Gerard. Holbein himself came here with an introduction Holbein
from Erasmus to Sir Thomas More in 1526, and here he
stayed till his death from the plague in 1543. Painter,
silversmith or at all events designer of silver-work, Holbein was architect as well, and to him are attributed the
gateways of Whitehall palace that have now disappeared. Whitehall gateways
They were purely English, however, with windows over
an archway between two octagonal turrets faced with flint
and stone, and with nothing foreign but some terra-cotta
roundels probably by Italians like those at Hampton Court.

In the case of the Royal Exchange in London the The Royal Exchange by Flemish architect
plan seems actually to have been given by a Flemish
architect. It was built by Sir Thomas Gresham after
1566, from the design it is said of Henry de Pas of
Antwerp. It perished in the great fire, but from an engraving by Hollar[2] it seems to have been a building of
two storeys surrounding a court with an attic in the roof.
The ground floor had an open arcade inwards; the upper
floor on the side to the courtyard had niches with statues
between pilasters, and there were dormers in the roof.
On one side was a lofty clock-tower. The general effect
is not unlike that of the house of Plantin and Moretus at
Antwerp; and some of the material, such as the black

[1] Walpole, *Anecdotes*, vol. I., speaks of Luke Gerard Horneband, but Luke
and Gerard seem to have been two persons.

[2] Reproduced by Sir Reginald Blomfield, *History of the Renaissance in
England*, vol I. p. 34.

and white marble with which the court was paved was imported by Sir Thomas Gresham from Flanders. From the Netherlands came the fashion of cut, scrolled, or curved gables which appear in Elizabethan architecture, and often superseded the simple English gable of Tudor times, not always to the advantage of the design. The fashion was not universally adopted however. In some cases the two forms are used alternately in the same design, or arranged as in S. John's House at Warwick where three plain gables are flanked at each end by a curved one, and in less important buildings the simple gable generally held its own against the innovation. I know no more charming example of a building of this period and of the smaller kind than the Old Hall at HAMBLETON in Rutland (Plate VIII) which combines a modest dignity with simplicity, and delicately refined detail with plain walling. Here the simple English gable survives.

The curved gable

Hambleton Old Hall

KIRBY HOUSE (Fig. 17) in Northamptonshire is, in many respects, the most beautiful building in this style. It is described by the County historian of 1791 as having been "built by the Stafford family, as appeareth from their crest, a boar's head out of a ducal coronet, and HUMFRE STAFFORD on several parts of it. Here are three orders of pillars: above the second order is this legend, IE SERAI 1572 LOYAL, and on the inner porch this date, 1638. The gardens here are beautiful, stocked with a great variety of exotic plants, and adorned with a wilderness composed of almost the whole variety of English trees, arranged in elegant order[1]."

Kirby House

Now, alas! Kirby, which was inhabited almost within living memory, is a melancholy ruin, buried in woods, a

Its ruinous state

[1] Whalley, *History of Northamptonshire*, 1791, vol. II. p. 314.

Plate VIII

HAMBLETON OLD HALL, RUTLAND

Plate IX

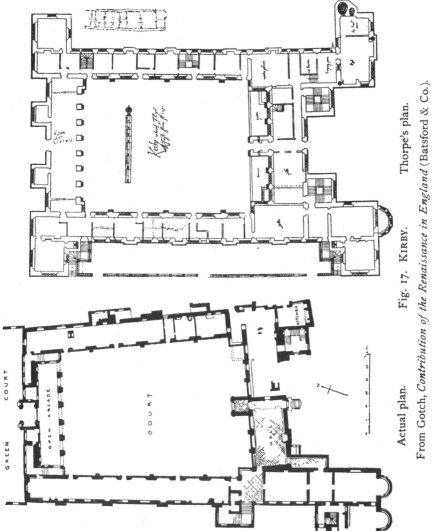

Actual plan.   Fig. 17. KIRBY.   Thorpe's plan.

From Gotch, *Contribution of the Renaissance in England* (Batsford & Co.).

Kirby

Altered by
Inigo
Jones

wilderness indeed, and not easy to find. It has been altered more than once, the last innovator being Inigo Jones, who formed the forecourt with its gateway and arcaded wall through which the house is approached ; he also modernized and spoilt the north front, and built a clock-tower on it, which has now disappeared ; he disfigured the inside of that building towards the quadrangle with classic windows, and replaced by a classic window of his own, that in the Tower over the entrance to the Hall and south block. This is no doubt the work to which the date 1638 refers.

The south block seems designed to stand complete without the side blocks. It has a fine central feature, a kind of tower, in which is the entrance to the Hall (Plate IX). On each side of the door and the window over it are coupled columns, Ionic below Corinthian above, and the design finishes with a curved gable faced with a row of little colonnettes and otherwise ornamented. Right and left of this are magnificent mullioned and transomed windows reaching the whole height of the building, with a break forward in each angle of the court. This break, were the side wings of the court not there, would make the south wing an E shaped block, and each of these two end projections has a gable on it, richly ornamented like the central one and evidently meant to be well seen though the roof of the side wing now runs into it and partly covers it, as if it were an afterthought. The splendid long windows of this south block are the distinguishing characteristic of Kirby, and the effect of the whole elevation is superb and I think unique[1] (Plate IX).

The Hall
wing

[1] It must be admitted that this effect is partly produced at the expense of consistency ; for though the windows to the right light the Hall, which is of the whole height of the building, those to the left are divided by a floor half way up.

Plate X

KIRBY

Plate XI

KIRBY—DOOR IN QUADRANGLE

SENAT CONS ANDRE
AE DE ORIA PATRIAE
LIBERATOR I MVNVS
PVBLICVM.

GENOA—DOOR OF HOUSE OF ANDREA DORIA

The west wing runs southward past the Hall block and finishes with two beautiful round bays of mullioned lights; and here in the gables cut and shaped into scrolls, with which they finish, we get the first touch of Dutch or Flemish influence (Plate X). Similar gables, alternating with finely designed chimney stacks are continued along the outside of the west wing. Those of the east wing are plainer, and there are no gables at all inwards towards the quadrangle in either wing. *The drawing room bays* *The curved gables*

The side wings are designed like a college, with doors and staircases at regular intervals, as it were a row of houses; obviously the best way of securing privacy in buildings with no continuous interior corridors.

In the quadrangle there is no trace of Flemish influence. What is not English is Italian. The doors (Plate XI) show a slight coarseness in the mouldings of the entablature, but they suggest that the architect must have seen some Italian doors, like that of the house at Genoa given by his grateful country to Andrea Doria, *liberatori Patriae* (Plate XI). The doors vary in detail though preserving the same general design. In their friezes occurs the Stafford crest of the boar's head issuing from a ducal crown; and there is the Stafford knot, the family badge, with the initials H.S. for Sir Humfrey Stafford of Blatherwyck who built the house between 1570 and 1575. Between the windows of the court the bays are divided by fluted pilasters with a kind of Ionic capital, except that right and left of the entrance in the north wing the shafts are carved with regular Italian arabesques, not perhaps up to the Florentine standard, but very fair. I imagine they are by English carvers working in the new manner (Plate XII). *Quadrangle English and Italian* *The arabesque*

A special interest attaches to Kirby from its connexion

John
Thorpe

with John Thorpe the architect to whom the well-known sketch book in Sir John Soane's museum belonged. It contains a ground plan of Kirby, with which the actual building generally, though not exactly agrees and Thorpe says of Kirby that he "layd yᵉ first stone 1570" (Fig. 17). But we must reserve John Thorpe for further notice here-

Beauty of
detail at
Kirby

after. The architect of Kirby whoever he may be was a man of genius. The building shows a degree of originality, and mastery of detail, together with a delicacy and refinement that raise Kirby above any other building of the style and date except perhaps Lyveden, which however shows far less imagination.

Longleat

LONGLEAT HOUSE in Somerset and Wilts (Plate XIII) is a little older than Kirby. It was built for Sir John Thynne between 1567 and 1579, and as is supposed from the designs

John of
Padua

of John of Padua, a mysterious person of whom we know even less than we do of John Thorpe. All that we do know of him in fact is that on June 24, 1544, he received a grant of 2s. a day from Henry VIII for his services in architecture and music[1], and that this grant was renewed by Edward VI in 1547 and 1548. Tradition connects him with Protector Somerset's house in the Strand as well as with Longleat, but there is no real proof of his connexion with either building. That some Italian was connected with the design of Longleat is suggested by the peculiarities of its style, and confirmed by entries in the accounts under the date of 1568, if we may take

[1] Rex etc. etc. sciatis quod nos, de gratia nostra speciali et ex certa scientia et mero motu nostris, necnon in consideratione boni et fidelis servitii quod dilectus serviens noster *Johannes de Padua* nobis in architectura ac aliis in re musica inventis impendit ac impendere intendit, dedimus et concessimus, etc. etc. He is further described as "devizer of his Majesty's buildings." Walpole's *Anecdotes* and *Dict. of National Biography*.

Plate XII

KIRBY

Plate XIII

LONGLEAT

Ganony to stand for some such name as *Giannone*, as *Torrysany* did for *Torrigiano*.

Prested to Adrian Ganony for the model xlv^s and to Robert Powell for carriage of stone in July xv.

and again,

Prest to Adrian Ganony xv^e of Aprill 1568 in part of payment for a more some for making of ye model for Langleat.

A model, as we have seen in former cases (Part i. *Italy*, pp. 54, 148) was the way of submitting a design[1], and it seems that a model or plan for building Longleat was made by one Adriano Giannone. May we then assume further that the design also was by this unknown artist, or must we suppose that he was only employed, like Brunelleschi's carpenter, to make the design for some one else, John of Padua or another? There is also a tradition that the plan of Longleat was intended for Protector Somerset, with whom Sir John Thynne had relations, and that Sir John used it when the Protector's fall made it useless to him. Whoever it was that made the design, the builder who carried it out seems to have been Robert Smythson whose name will occur again when we come to Wollaton in Nottinghamshire. In a letter to Sir John Thynne on March 11, 1568, Sir Humfrey Lovell recommends

This berer Robert Smytheson, fremason, who of laytt was with Master Vice Chamberlaine, not dowting hem boutt to be a man fett for youre worshepe and with these covenantes : fyrste he to have xvi^d a daye holle that ys to say viij^s a weke and a nage kepte at your worshepes charges,

---

[1] The model was not necessarily a constructional one such as those made for Brunelleschi for instance, but was sometimes a drawing on paper, in which sense Shakespeare uses the word:

when we mean to build
We first survey the plot, then draw the model.
Henry IV, Part ii. Act i. sc. iii.

Longleat

and the reste of hes men xii^d a daye. Seconde hes men to have dayes wages for theare travell that ys to say xij^d a daye wheles thaye are in comenge, and the carriage of theare towles pade for and hemselfe ys contented to stand to youre worshepes benevolence trowsting youe welle conseder of hem[1].

Italian character of Longleat

Longleat has a more distinctly Italian character than the other great houses of the same date. While it is less Gothic than Kirby it is also free from the Flemish touch that we find there. It is decorated outside with classic columns, each storey separately, and finishes with a level cornice unbroken by gables, and with a flat roof hidden by the parapet, on which are statues. The Italian details have no doubt lost something of their purity in the hands of Robert Smythson and his English workmen, but Longleat is more like an Italian palace than any of the other great Elizabethan mansions. The present unbroken facade however appears to be different from what was originally proposed, for at the back the roof shows a range of gables which seem intended to run through to the front; and there are even signs that they may have actually done so and been afterwards removed for the greater convenience of the gallery which occupies the top storey.

The flat roof

The gallery at Longleat has been partitioned for purpose of housing Bishop Ken's library, but originally it ran unbroken along the front. A gallery in the top storey was a regular feature in the Elizabethan house. At Montacute it runs from end to end of the building. At Knole it runs round two sides of the quadrangle. At Grove Place in Hampshire it occupies the whole top floor. At Audley End there was a magnificent gallery which Evelyn pronounced the best in England. It was a place for children

The Elizabethan gallery

---

[1] I am indebted to the kindness of the Marquis of Bath for these extracts from letters and papers at Longleat.

to play in, and for their elders to take exercise. Wolsey's Wolsey's
galleries galleries at Hampton Court "fayre, both large and long" were famous, and Edward VI complained of Windsor that there were no galleries, and he felt like a prisoner. The long gallery in the colleges at Cambridge is a feature of the Master's house. That at Queens' College forms a beautiful feature, and there is another at Emmanuel. They were decorated with good plaster ceilings, heraldry, and painted glass, were well lit, and had fireplaces. Fig. 18 shows one that exists in the gallery at Longleat[1].

The gallery at Cambridge

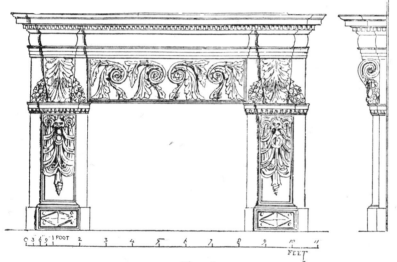

Fig. 18.

Sir Richard Colt Hoare says the house was finished in 1580, and he quotes the following items of the cost of building from account books[2]:—

Cost of building at Longleat

---

[1] This was hidden behind a lath and plaster partition, and discovered during the recent repairs of the Hall roof and ceiling. I believe if further search were made others might be found.

[2] *History of Modern Wiltshire*, vol. I. p. 64. But this sum cannot cover the whole cost of the building, comparing it with the £80,000 spent on Wollaton and £190,000 at Audley End.

Longleat

The first booke.   Three years lacking three weeks
    from 21 Jan. 1567 to the last of December 1570   *li.* 2780.   2.   5¾
Second booke.   Being five years from 1st January
    1571 to the last of December 1575   ...   ...   *li.* 3755.   1.   2½
Third, fourth and fifth books from 1st January 1576
    to yᵉ 29 of March 1578 ...   .   *li.* 1481. 10.   0

                                            li. 8016. 13.   8¼

But as mention is made of a fire that burned for
several hours on 21 April 1567 the house must have
been begun more than 3 months before then, or there
would have been nothing to burn.

CHAPTER VI

THE MIDDLE RENAISSANCE (*continued*)

THERE were two inconveniences in the Tudor and early Elizabethan houses, compared with our modern buildings, so obvious and so easily avoided that one wonders why the remedy was so long deferred.

The first is the want of interior communication by corridors. In a few cases, as in the base court at Hampton Court, there is a corridor from which the rooms open, and this was the plan in monastic buildings, except the Charterhouses, where each monk had a little house to himself with a garden attached. But in most houses of the 16th and 17th centuries the rooms were all passage rooms, and on the upper floors if not so much on the ground floor, the inconvenience would to us seem intolerable. But our forefathers made very little provision for privacy in planning their houses. In several cases interior corridors have since been formed, as for instance at Burghley. In the Colleges at Oxford and Cambridge another plan is adopted. The lodgings round the court consist of separate houses, each with its own entrance and stairs rising in a ramp from floor to floor. The rooms of the Brethren in the Hospital at S. Cross near Winchester, and in numerous similar establishments, follow the same plan. At the Universities this arrangement may have been inherited from the Halls which preceded the Colleges, and which consisted of two or three or more adjoining houses hired by the Master from the townsmen. Indeed the conventual plan seems purposely avoided at the Universities, where there was no love for the Regular orders. At Kirby it would seem from the numerous doors at regular intervals in the court that the collegiate plan of separate blocks was adopted, and that at each doorway there was a staircase with rooms right and left on each of the two floors. Failing the interior corridor the collegiate plan makes the best provision for privacy, and the necessity of going out of doors from one part of the building to another is only what every member of a college experiences. The Master of the house and his family of course lived in the main central block, and the wings were occupied by retainers, guests, or servants.

The newel staircase in domestic use   The second inconvenience was the absence of good easy staircases. The newel, or cork-screw stair, by which we climb a church tower, was the type also of all staircases in domestic buildings during the Middle Ages and well into the 16th century. Sometimes they were wide and spacious, as at Blois and Chambord, where they are on a monumental scale : but generally a width of 3 or 4 feet was thought to be a handsome allowance even in considerable mansions. In stone districts, they were usually of stone, but elsewhere often of wood, the steps sometimes made

Eastbury House   of solid blocks. Eastbury House, near Barking in Essex, built in 1572, has two newel stairs of this kind, with steps of solid oak. The house is built of red brick surrounding a small courtyard on three sides, and the stairs are contained in octagonal turrets in the two inner angles of the court[1].

Grove Place   Eastbury house is falling into neglect and ruin, but a beautiful example of the same plan exists at Grove Place in Hampshire (Fig. 19). The two turret stairs are placed

[1] For account and illustrations of this house see Garner and Stratton, *Tudor architecture*.

Plate XIV

T. G. J.

GROVE PLACE—STAIRCASE

as at Eastbury in the re-entering angles of the court, which here is on a larger scale, and is open on the fourth side. The stairs in the right-hand turret, which are of solid oak, The two turret stairs instead of a newel have a winding string round a small well (Plate XIV). The other staircase has a square well, enclosed by partitions in which it is said there was a small lift, so far as I know an unique instance of such a con- The lift trivance in an Elizabethan house. Unhappily it no longer

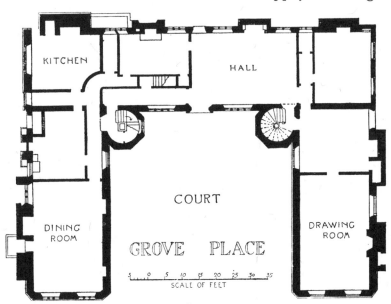

Fig. 19.

exists. Grove Place, which was built between 1570 and 1581 by James Pagett, son of a London Alderman[1], is a well-preserved example of a manor house of the period,

[1] From 1570–1604 James Pagett appears in the Court Rolls of the Manor of Southwells, to which Grove Place belongs, as joint Lord with the Dean and Chapter of Windsor, the owners, from whom he held it. The arms of Bridget Mill, his second wife, appear in the plaster ceilings, but not those of the third wife whom he married in 1581.—B. W. Greenfield. Paper read to the Hants. Field Club, May 8, 1895.

and of the second grade in point of magnitude (Fig. 20). It has fine plaster ceilings and over-mantels, and at the top a long gallery in the roof running the whole length of the central block with a gable and window at each end. It is built of a sober red brick, with grey headers in diapers, and stone is economized as much as possible in the dressings.

It was not till the latter half of the 16th century that more convenient staircases came to be constructed. The early examples are enclosed in square chambers of ample dimensions, round which the stairs run in straight flights with square landings in the angles, leaving a square well in the middle. The Bodleian Library at Oxford has a square chamber in each corner of the quadrangle for a staircase of this kind. At each corner of the well a post could be placed to support the landing above and the ramp that sprang from it. These posts were formed into columns and handsomely finished. But the angle posts before long were abandoned and a newel post with a figure of man or beast or an ordinary finial took their place at each turn of the stairway. As these afforded no support to the part above, staircases so constructed have generally sunk more or less inwards towards the well, the indirect support given by the meeting of the ramps and landing being insufficient.

In John Thorpe's plan of Kirby (Fig. 17, p. 69) two staircases are shown in square chambers at the back of the Hall-block, though only one appears in the plan that was executed. There is a good example of the chambered staircase in the old manor house of Pyrton in Oxfordshire. An early instance of it occurs at Barrington Court, which dates from the middle of the 16th century; there is another at Lytes-Cary and one of a later date at Aston

Fig. 20.

T.G.J.

Hall[1]. The staircases by degrees came out into the open
instead of being enclosed in a chamber, and at Burghley
is an example of what has been called the Roman staircase,
scala Romana, where a solid wàll divides the two ramps
that run contraryways to reach the upper floor, each ramp
being ceiled with a waggon vault decorated with coffering
and rosettes[2].

The need of more ready còmmunication in the interior
of the house than the old winding turret stairs afforded
naturally became imperative as the houses grew to the
enormous dimensions of those built in the Tudor and
Elizabethan periods. The numerous retinue of servants
and retainers demanded to be better housed than they
had been in the middle ages, when they slept on the
rushes of the Hall floor with their feet to the fire, and
when no one but the master or member of his family had
a room to himself[3]. Wolsey's household, as we have seen,
consisted of five hundred persons of whom Cavendish
gives a detailed list with their several offices. Thomas
Sackville, the first Earl of Dorset, and High Treasurer
of England, had a household of two hundred persons.
There exists a curious catalogue of the household of
Richard, the third Earl of Dorset, at Knole early in the
17th century, with the place of each person at the tables
of the Hall. My Lord and Lady with their family and a
few principal inmates, eight persons in all, sit at the High
table. At the Parlour table are twenty-one persons, in-

The open staircase

Occasion for better communication

Size of Tudor and Elizabethan families

Household at Knole

[1] *The Lyte's of Lyte's Cary*, by Sir H. Maxwell Lyte. Niven's *Monograph of Aston Hall*.

[2] Illustrated from Richardson by Gotch, *Early Renaissance in England*.

[3] At Little Wenham Hall, in Suffolk, which goes back to the 13th century, a vaulted hall 37 ft. long on the ground floor, with another above it, a chapel, and two small rooms without fireplaces, formed the whole accommodation for a knightly establishment.

cluding the Chaplain, Gentleman-usher, the Secretary and pages, Mr Mathew Caldicott my Lord's favourite, the Steward and six ladies. At the Clerks' table are the Cooks, the yeomen of the Buttery and Pantry, the Baker, the Brewer, the Slaughterer, the Gardeners, the Groom of the Wardrobe, and Lowy, a French boy; in all twenty-one persons. At the Nursery table were Nurse Carpenter and three more. The Long Table in the Hall accommodated My Lord's attendants, the Groom of my Lord's Bedchamber, My Lady Margaret's man, Grooms and footmen, in all forty-seven. At the Laundry-maids' table sat William Lewis the Porter and eleven women, including the Lady Margaret's maid, the Dairymaid, and Grace Robinson a blackamoor. At the Kitchen and Scullery table sat six men including John Morockoe a blackamoor[1].

All these men and women would have been inmates of the mansions, but even their numbers do not account for the magnitude of a great Elizabethan house. It was an age of display and magnificence, and every one of these Elizabethan palaces was furnished with state rooms, parlours, and galleries, not for domestic use but for great entertainments, and the visits possibly of royalty, by which Queen Elizabeth impoverished many of her favourites. Lord Treasurer Burghley, besides his great house near Stamford, had of necessity his house in London of which the memory is preserved by Exeter Hall and the names of several streets in the Strand; and in 1563 he bought the estate of Theobalds at Cheshunt in Hertfordshire where he built a famous house which has now disappeared. It was intended for his younger son Robert, and built at

---

[1] Bridgman, *Historical and Topographical Sketch of Knole*, p. 79. I think this catalogue sufficiently curious to be given in full in an appendix at the end of this chapter. The gradation of the hierarchy of service is interesting.

Theobalds first "but for a little Pile"; but it grew to a palace for the entertainment of Queen Elizabeth, at whose instance Burghley was induced to prolong his great gallery to still further dimensions[1]. King James fell in love with Theobalds and induced Sir Robert Cecil to exchange it for Hatfield; and at Theobalds he died in 1625. Theobalds was only

Holdenby and Sir Christopher Hatton

His purchase of Kirby

equalled in size by Audley End, and Holdenby. Of the latter house there are hardly any remains. It was built by Sir Christopher Hatton, who, not contented with one of the largest mansions in the kingdom, bought Kirby from the Staffords on the death of Sir Humphrey in 1580. He had not even been to see it, for he writes to his friend Sir Thomas Heneage in that year

"I have determined to take my pilgrimage to Sir Ed. Bricknell's (Brudenell's) to view my house of Kirby which I never yet surveyed, leaving my other shrine, I mean Holdenbye, still unseen until that holy Saint may sit in it, to whom it is dedicated."

The extravagant scale of some of these buildings, and the splendour of the entertainments for which they were de-

Impoverishment of the noble

vised, impoverished many of the noblemen and others who built them. Burghley was troubled by doubts of his son's capacity to maintain himself at Theobalds. The honour of a visit from the Queen, who was fond of staying at her subjects' houses, cost them dearly. She was more than once at Theobalds, and each visit cost Cecil from £2000 to £3000. We can imagine that it was with a suppressed sigh that he writes to Sir Christopher Hatton about their two houses, Holdenby and Burghley, "God send us both long to enjoy Her for whom we both meant to exceed our purses in these." Although it does not appear that the "holy Saint" did ever pay the expected visit to Holdenby,

[1] There is a plan of Theobalds in Gotch's *Homes of the Cecils*, reconstructed from that in John Thorpe's book. No real representation of the house is known to exist.

Hatton is said to have been killed by her insisting on his repaying money which he owed to the Crown. For most modern domestic establishments these great mansions, covering acres of ground are a world too wide : many of them like Audley End have been reduced by pulling down courts or wings, and in others the state apartments have become something like a museum, shown to visitors, but not regularly lived in by the family.

AUDLEY END in its prime was perhaps the largest of these private mansions, unless Holdenby was greater still. It was begun in 1603 by Thomas Howard, who was created Earl of Suffolk in that year, and Lord High Treasurer in 1614. The house was finished in 1616, and is said to have cost £190,000, an enormous sum at that date. The design according to tradition was brought from Italy and cost £500 : but there is little if anything about the house either in architecture or decoration that speaks of Italian influence. The original plan appears in John Thorpe's book. He shows an immense court, with the main buildings of the Hall and its two porches facing the entrance, and a colonnaded wing right and left. The offices lay off to one side in a separate wing, and behind the main block was a second court, with other buildings beyond it again. Evelyn, who saw the house in its prime in 1654, describes it as a "mixt fabric 'twixt antiq and modern, but observable for its being completely finish'd, and it is one of the stateliest palaces in the kingdom. It consists of two courts, the first very large and winged with cloisters." The gallery he says is "most cheerfull," and he thinks it one of the best in England[1]. Either in

---

[1] Evelyn, *Diary*, Aug. 31, 1654. See also Pepys, *Diary*, Feb. 27, 1659–60, and Oct. 7, 1667.

1700, or 1749 according to others, the great court and part of the other were pulled down, and the house was reduced to the central block which still forms a great mansion. With the rest disappeared Evelyn's "cheerfull gallery," which is said to have been 236 feet long, 32 wide, and 24 feet high, a noble promenade and play-room in wet weather.

The two porches are the most striking features of the exterior (Plate XV). They are richly decorated with columns and friezes of marble, apparently Italian, and this may explain the legend of the Italian plan of the house, for the rest of the building is in the regular sober English style of mullioned and transomed architecture. The details of the porches are heavily profiled, and the columns seem oppressed by their loads. The proportions of the parapets of the upper order, and the pedestals on which the columns rest would not have satisfied an Italian eye. Bernard Jansen, a Flemish architect, is said to have been employed, and to him these rather ponderous porches may perhaps be attributed. John Thorpe is supposed to have worked with him. Our English climate has revenged itself on the intrusion of an un-English material, and has corroded the marble till it looks no better than common stone. The interior of the house is rich in plastered ceilings and carved chimney pieces, and interwoven with the Renaissance ornament are quatrefoil panels of the half-forgotten Gothic art. Half forgotten, but never wholly forgotten, for even after it ceased to exist as a style it continued to influence and modify its successor.

The picturesque old Guildhall in the High Street of EXETER is another example of the heavy-handed way in which the Elizabethans managed the features of the new style which they were striving to make their own.

Plate XV

AUDLEY END

Plate XVI

WOLLATON HOUSE

WOLLATON HOUSE near Nottingham (Plate XVI) is
older than Audley End, and a little later than Kirby. It was
begun by Sir Francis Willoughby in 1580 and finished in
1588, as an inscription over the Garden door records. The
plan is peculiar; a great Hall in the middle, 52 ft. high is
girdled on all sides by wings containing rooms, with a
square pavilion at each angle attached to the main quadrangular block at one corner only. The Hall, in order to
be lighted, rises above the surrounding wings and has
another room above. This great overpowering central
building swamps the house proper which encircles it, and
spoils the design. Symmetry rules the plan: all four sides
are treated decoratively, and are of equal consequence,
and as Mr Gotch points out the offices have to be in
a basement in order not to mar the architectural effect.
He quotes an account of the house written in 1702, by
Cassandra Willoughby, Duchess of Chandos; she says
"Yᵉ master-workmen which built yᵉ House he" (Sir Francis
Willoughby) "sent for out of Italy, as also most of yᵉ
Stone figures which adorn yᵉ house. All yᵉ stone which
it is built with was brought from Ancaster, in Lincolnshire,
by yᵉ people who dwelt there, and who exchanged their
Stone with Sir Francis for his Cole." She adds that the
house cost fourscore thousand pounds[1].

In spite of this account, written 114 years after the
house was finished, the building shows no trace of direct
Italian design. There are busts in roundels of Classic
worthies, but Classic allusion was fashionable then in
England and they may after all be carved by Englishmen. Italian statues however were to have filled the
niches, but they were lost, according to tradition, by the
wreck of a ship that was bringing them from Italy. The
top windows of the lofty central block have traceries

[1] Gotch, *Architecture of the Renaissance in England*, vol. II. p. 62.

Wollaton something like those at the Scuola di S. Rocco, and the Cornér-Spinelli and Vendramin-Calergi palaces at Venice (Part I. *Italy*, Plates XXVI, XXVII, XXIX). Beyond this the whole work shows no Italian feeling. The windows are mullioned and transomed, and the pilasters and cornices, with which the building is plentifully furnished, are such as had by that time become usual in English Renaissance masonry.

The pilasters are heavy and both they and the columns have a broad flat band half way up, almost a rustication, which is unpleasant. Both they and the elaborate brattisching which surmounts the angle pavilions seem to speak of Flemish or German extraction, and certainly have nothing akin to Italian work. In the church

Monument of Robert Smythson of Wollaton is a monument with this epitaph.

"HERE LYETH Y^E BODY OF MR ROBERT SMYTHSON, GENT. ARCHITECTOR AND SVRVAYOR VNTO THE MOST WORTHY HOVSE OF WOLLATON WITH DIVERS OTHERS OF GREAT ACCOVNT HE LIVED IN Y^E FAYTH OF CHRIST 79 YEARS & THEN DEPARTED THIS LIFE Y^E XV OF OCTOBER ANŌ DM̄I 1614."

This is probably the same Robert Smythson of whom we heard at Longleat (v. *sup*. p. 73) where he was described as a *fremason*, and the arms on his monument, according to Mr Gotch, are those of the Mason's company[1]. How far he was the designer of the building may be questioned. The word "Architect" was used in those days in a wide sense for merely builder. The architect in our sense of the word was only just beginning to be developed.

[1] The arms are a compass expanded between three castles.

APPENDIX

A CATALOGUE

Of the Household and Family of the Right Honourable Richard Earl of House-
Dorset, in the Year of our Lord 1613, and so continued until the Year 1624 hold at
at Knole in Kent &c to which was added a Prayer for the Family. Knole

AT MY LORD'S TABLE

My Lord ; my Lady ; my Lady Margaret ; my Lady Isabella ; Mr
Sackville ; Mr Frost ; John Musgrave ; Thomas Garret.

AT THE PARLOUR TABLE

Mrs Field ; Mrs Willoughby ; Mrs Grimsditch ; Mrs Stewkly ; Mrs
Fletcher; Mrs Wood; Mr Dupper, Chaplain; Mr Mathew Caldicott, my
Lord's favourite; Mr Edward Legge, Steward; Mr Peter Basket, Gentle-
man of the Horse; Mr Marsh, Attendant on my Lady; Mr Wooldridge;
Mr Cheyney; Mr Duck, Page; Mr Josiah Cooper, a Frenchman, Page;
Mr John Belgrave, Page ; Mr Billingsley ; Mr Graverner, Gentleman
Usher ; Mr Marshall, Auditor ; Mr Edwards, Secretary ; Mr Drake,
Attendant.

AT THE CLERKS' TABLE IN THE HALL

Edward Fulks, and John Edwards, Clerks of the Kitchen ; Edward
Care, Master Cook; William Smith, Yeoman of the Buttery; Henry
Keble, Yeoman of the Pantry ; John Michall, Pastry-man ; Thomas
Vinson, John Elnor, and Ralph Hussey, Cooks ; John Avery, Usher of
the Hall; Robert Elnor, Slaughterman; Benjamin Staples, Groom of the
Great Chamber; Thomas Petley, Brewer; William Turner, Baker ;
Francis Steeling and Richard Wicking, Gardeners ; Thomas Clements,
Under Brewer ; Samuel Vans, Caterer ; Edward Small, Groom of the
Wardrobe ; Samuel Souther, Under Baker ; Lowy, a French boy.

THE NURSERY

Nurse Carpenter; Widow Ben ; Jane Sisley; Dorothy Pickenden.

AT THE LONG TABLE IN THE HALL

Robert Care, Attendant on my Lord; Mr Gray, Attendant likewise;
Mr Roger Cook, Attendant on my Lady Margaret; Mr Adam Bradford,
Barber; Mr John Guy, Groom of my Lord's Bedchamber; Walter Come-
stone, Attendant on my Lady ; Edward Lane, Scrivener ; Mr Thomas
Poor, Yeoman of the Wardrobe ; Mr Thomas Lennard, Master Hunts-
man ; Mr Woodgate, Yeoman of the Great Chamber ; John Hall,

Falconer; James Flennel, Yeoman of the Granary; Rawlinson, Armourer; Moses Shonk, Coachman; Anthony Ashby, Groom of the Great Horse; Griffin Edwards, Groom of my Lady's Horse; Francis Turner, Groom of the Great Horse; William Grymes, Groom of the Great Horse; Acton Curvett, chief Footman; James Loveall, Footman; Sampson Ashley, Footman; William Petley, Footman; Nicholas James, Footman; Paschal Beard, Footman; Elias Thomas, Footman; Henry Spencer, Farrier; Edward Goodsall; John Sant, the Steward's man; Ralph Wise, Groom of the Stables; Thomas Petley, Under Farrier; John Stephens, the Chaplain's man; John Haite, Groom for the Stranger's Horse; Thomas Giles, Groom of the Stables; Richard Thomas, Groom of the Hall; Christopher Wood, Groom of the Pantry; George Owen and George Vigeon, Huntsmen; Thomas Grittan, Groom of the Buttery; Solomon, the Bird-catcher; Richard Thornton, the Coachman's man; Richard Pickenden, Postilion; William Roberts, groom; the Armourer's man; Ralph Wise, his Servant; John Swift, the Porter's man; John Atkins and Clement Doory, men to carry wood.

THE LAUNDRY MAIDS' TABLE

Mrs Judith Simpton; Mrs Grace Simpton; Penelope Tutty, the Lady Margaret's Maid; Anne Mills, Dairy-maid; Prudence Bucher; Anne Howse; Faith Husband; Elinor Thompson; Goodwife Burton; Grace Robinson, a Blackamoor; Goodwife Small; William Lewis, Porter.

KITCHEN AND SCULLERY

Diggory Dyer; Marfidy Snipt; John Watson; Thomas Harman; Thomas Johnson; John Morockoe, a Blackamoor.

SERVANTS AT DORSET HOUSE, LONDON

John Justice, Porter; Henry and George Grindall, Wardrobe; John Lane, Grainery-man; William Wellins, Gardener; Thomas Call, Farrier; Goodwife Mowberry; Elizabeth Dorey, Keeper of the Sick.

BOLEBROOK HOUSE, SUSSEX

William Gardener; Thomas Gilbert, Keeper.

CHAPTER VII

THE MIDDLE RENAISSANCE (*continued*)

JOHN THORPE who has been mentioned several times already, is almost as mysterious a personage as John of Padua, with whom it was at one time sought to identify him. He was discovered by Horace Walpole to whom the Earl of Warwick showed and gave a book which is now at Sir John Soane's Museum in Lincoln's Inn Fields. It is a folio neatly bound in dark brown leather and contains 280 pages of plans and sketches of Architecture on paper. They mostly relate to contemporary buildings of the Elizabethan and Jacobean time, but among them are drawings very neatly executed of the five classic orders, and there is a plan of Henry VII's chapel at Westminster which was built before Thorpe could have been born. The sheets are not all of a size, and in some cases the drawings are mounted. They are not all by the same hand; and in those towards the end of the book the writing is of a later character, and the word "*bed-chamber*" appears instead of *lodging* as in the earlier plans. Mr Campbell Dodgson in the *Dictionary of National Biography* and Mr Gotch both think the drawings were made in the book, and not collected and bound together; but the book does not give me that impression, nor does the binding seem so old as the time of Elizabeth and James I.

Near the beginning of the book is the plan of a house like the letters I and T connected by a hyphen. It is followed by a perspective of the ground plan

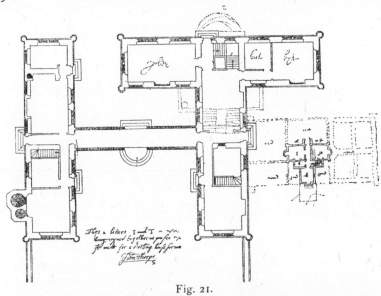

Fig. 21.

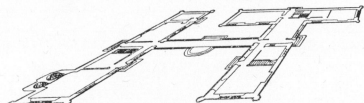

Fig. 22. From Gotch, *Architecture of the Renaissance in England.*
(Batsford and Co.)

(Figs. 21 and 22), and a sketch of the building. Underneath is written,

> Thes 2 letters I and **T**
> ~~being~~ joyned together as you ſee
> Js ment for a dwelling houſe for mee
> John Thorpe.

The sketch (Fig. 22) represents a considerable house
of three storeys and an attic, with simple curved gable
ends, the hyphen being a bridge of open timber work on
the first floor, with a passage also below. The I was intended for servants quarters, and the **T** for the family
residence. It does not appear whether the I-**T** house ever
got beyond this design on paper.

Except in this instance the plans in Thorpe's book do
not show much originality, but conform to the traditional
arrangement of a hall as the heart of the establishment,
approached through a screened passage with buttery and
offices on the other side. Very few of the drawings are
signed, but most of them seem by the handwriting, to be
Thorpe's. There is a great number of ground plans with
comparatively few elevations; some of them are named,
and others have been identified, but there are many about
which we know nothing: they may have been made
merely for amusement or practice in design. Among
those houses of which the drawings are either named
or have been recognized, are, Old Somerset House,
Buckhurst, Copt-Hall, Kirby, Wollaton, Burghley by
Stamford, Burley on the Hill, Sir W. Coap's house at
Kensington, now known as Holland House, Knole, Loseley,
Wimbledon House for Sir T. Cecil, Longford, Aston
Hall, Holdenby, Audley End and others. Horace Walpole concluded that he had discovered the architect of
most of the famous mansions of the late Elizabethan and

early Jacobean periods. Other writers, however, will have it that Thorpe was not an architect at all, but only a surveyor employed to measure existing buildings. That surveys of that kind did come within the range of his practice is proved by his appointment as commissioner to survey the Duchess of Suffolk's land in 1609. In 1590 he made a plan of the Palace at Eltham. In 1606 he received a "further" payment of £70. 8s. 8d. for surveying the house and lands at Holdenby, "with his own pains and three others a long time employed in drawing down and writing fair the plots of that and of Ampthill House and the Earl of Salisbury's by commandment of the Lord Treasurer of England." In 1611 he was paid £52. 3s. 0d. for repairs to the fence of Richmond Park. It has been suggested that these later entries and others down to 1618 refer not to him but to his son, another John Thorpe who is mentioned in the following extract from John

Peacham's *Gentleman's Exercise*, published in 1612. Peacham was a student of Heraldry, about which he writes at length in his other book, *The Compleat Gentleman*, and after describing a coat of arms, he says it is now borne by

John Thorpe of the parish of St Martin's in the Fields, my especial friend, and excellent geometrician and surveiour, whom the rather I remember because he is not only learned and ingenuous himself, but a furtherer and favourer of all excellency whatsoever, of whom our age findeth too few. And lastly the aforenamed Master John Thorpe his sonne, to whom I can in words never bee sufficiently thankfull.

To suppose on the authority of this book that John Thorpe built or designed all the houses of which it contains plans is not necessary or reasonable. The book is an album or note book in which are collected studies for his own use, such as the five orders and the chapel at Westminster already mentioned, together with a certain number of designs of his own, of which we shall speak presently, and others in which he was interested. In some cases it is not even pretended that the drawings represent actual buildings. In one case he writes against a drawing "a front or a garden syde for a nobleman." Again two of the elevations are copied from a French book of designs by Du Cerceau, *Les plus excellents bastiments de France* (published 1576–79), though Thorpe has embellished them with some fanciful dormers of a Dutch character. Another elevation is taken from a Flemish book by Jan Vrederman de Vries, published at Antwerp in 1577, to which Thorpe has also made additions. These would be studies made for his own information. But in certain cases he says pretty clearly that the building in question is wholly or partly his. He writes on the plan of Kirby (Fig. 17, p. 69 *sup.*)

Kerby whereof I layd yᵉ first stone Aᵒ 1570.

Against the plan of Holland House, then built for Sir William Cope, he writes "perfected by me—J. T." Of Ampthill old house he says "enlarged p. J. Thorpe[1]." In 1600 he was in France, and he gives a plan of the "*Queene Mother's house fabor S. Jarmines alla Paree,*" of which he says it was "altred p. J. Thorpe[2]." These notes imply that he acted as architect to those buildings; and this is confirmed by the fact that in minor particulars his plans differ from the actual structure. At Kirby for instance he shows two great chambered staircases, of which only one ever existed. He has drawn the court square, as he naturally would, but in fact it is narrower at the far end than at the house. The drawing room wing has two

---

[1] Sir R. Blomfield suggests that this means the drawing was enlarged from a smaller one. But it is only a small drawing now, and there would be no point in recording the mere re-drawing of a smaller plan.

[2] Elsewhere he has "Mounsier Jammet in Paris his howse, 1600," and in another place "Sᵗ Jarmins howse v leagues from Paris Aᵒ 1600."

Discrepan-
cies
between
book and
building
round bay windows (Plate X) where Thorpe only draws
one. And this one is an afterthought, drawn over the
square end which was once intended. There are similar
discrepancies in other cases between the plan and the
building as it was carried out, which is sufficient to
prove that the plans are not surveys of existing buildings, for if they were there would be none of these in-
accuracies. They are just such departures from the
original plan as would occur while the building was in
progress: they happen constantly in our own practice,
and must have been more frequent when there were
no complete working drawings, no detailed specifications,
no quantities, and no building contract beyond the
vaguest description of what the building was to be like.
Such a plan as Thorpe's would have been enough for
the master mason to set out the walls, and the general
design would be explained by model, or word of mouth,
as the building progressed, a great deal being left to the
master mason and workmen who followed the traditions of the craft in which they had been brought up.

The
modern
architect
then
unknown
The
master
mason
Before John Thorpe's day there were no architects of
the modern kind, who designed every detail of a building
and left nothing to the initiative of the workmen. The
real architect was the master mason who often worked
with his own hands, besides employing men to work
under him in addition to the general staffs of workmen, and

Wadham
College
building
accounts
in many cases he was contractor as well. Wadham College
at Oxford, has fortunately preserved the whole building
account of the structure from April 9, 1610, when
Mrs Wadham's "plows" of oxen started from Merifield
in Somerset to go by way of Yeovil, Amesbury, Hunger-
ford and Abingdon to Oxford, down to the consecration
of the chapel, and inauguration of the new foundation

with a prodigious feast in the Hall on April 29, 1613. Wadham College
The name of every man with his weekly wage, and the
work on which he was engaged is duly recorded, but there
is no mention of any architect, nor even of any model
having been made as at Longleat. The head workman
William Arnoll or Arnold received £1 a week, evidently William Arnold
for design and superintendence, and besides this he had
three free-masons, or workers of free-stone under him,
described as *his men*, for whose work he was paid, and
on which he no doubt made a profit[1]. This was the mediaeval plan, when the *Lapicida, capo-maestro, maître,
master-mason*, lived at the work, laboured manually,
executed part at all events of the sculpture, and bound
himself to undertake no other work till this was finished.
These men were the real architects, or rather architects
and clerks of the works in one, to whom the details and
general working out of the design was due, though of
course the general scheme, scale, and arrangement of the
buildings was given them by the employer, as in fact it is
to the architect of to-day. They seem to have attained to The master mason as architect
fame and reputation, rising gradually as they were em-
ployed on greater things. Of William Arnold I am sorry
to find no further trace, but as Somerset abounds in fine
domestic architecture in the style and of the date of
Wadham, some of the buildings we admire in that county

[1] v. my *History of Wadham College*, ch. II. p. 33. I give in an appendix
at the end of this chapter a few extracts from the MS. account of the building
expenses. The total cost of the College, including part of the painted glass,
desks and 12 dozen chains for the books, pots and pans for the kitchen, and
£100 to start the Bursars, was £11,360. Omitting these extraneous items, it
appears that in the time of James I a public building could be erected at the
rate of 2½d. per cubic foot. The rate for collegiate and University buildings
at Oxford before the late war, in my own experience, ranged from 1s. to 1s. 2d.
This agrees with the usual estimate that the difference between the purchasing
power of money in the time of James I and now was about 5 to 1.

may be by his hand. Robert Smythson, employed as a
free-mason at Longleat between 1567 and 1579[1] reappears
in 1580 at Wollaton, and at his death in 1614 is described
as *Architector and Survayor* of that house and divers
others of great account. Thomas Holt of York who contracted as *fabor lignarius*, for the woodwork of the new
Quadrangle at Merton College in 1608, and made the
fine hammer-beam roof of the hall at Wadham College
in 1611, was architect of the Schools Quadrangle for
Sir Thomas Bodley in 1613, and when he died in 1629
his skill as an artist was lauded on his tomb in Holywell
Churchyard in Latin Iambics[2], that recall the elegy by an
Italian poetess on Palladio, who she says had gone to
heaven to improve the architecture there[3].

In the time of John Thorpe, however, we see the
first signs of a transition. The old manner of managing
building operations begins to give way and shows a
tendency towards the professional architect of a few years
later, and of our own time. Gentlemen intending to build
may have consulted Thorpe and other men like him, and
obtained sketch-plans and elevations, but having got them
they would pass them on to the actual builders, so that
in many cases the author of the design would have no
superintendence of the work. This may account for the
strange differences in style shown by the various houses
of which there is any reason to attribute the ground plan
to Thorpe. For exact instructions as to detail we know
that recourse was had in some cases directly to the employer and not to any professional architect. Roger Warde,
mason, writes from *Burlaye* on June xiii, 1556, to

---

[1] v. *supra*, pp. 73, 74.

[2] THO. HOLT. Ebor. Scholarum Public. Architecti obt Sept. 9. 1624.
The epitaph will be found in Peshall's *Wood. Appendix*, p. 25. The tombstone
has disappeared.   [3] v. Part I. of this work, *Italy*, p. 172.

Sir William Cecil that he cannot understand from John Mores how his worship would have his *lukons*, or dormer windows. He says, " I shall dyssyer yowe to drawe youre menynge how and after what facyon yowe wolde have them to be made in all poynts bothe the wyde of the lyght and also the heght of the same, wythe the fassyon of all the molds thatt dowthe belonge there unto." Sir William is further asked to give him dimensions for the steps up to the terrace. Also he says " I shar dyssyer yowe to drawe a tryke of youre plessewre in all thyngs y^t ye wolde that I shulde dowe[1]." Burghley House. Details by the Employer

This is an instance when we may imagine a general plan, with probably an elevation or two, drawn by John Thorpe, or someone of the same profession, to the satisfaction of the employer, was carried out without any further professional superintendence. On the other hand some of the drawings in Thorpe's book have corrections, and alterations marked on them which seem to prove that in those cases his control over the design did not cease with the bare preliminary sketches. I have mentioned those at Kirby. In the elevations, or " uprights " as he calls them of Wollaton the little vedettes as they might be styled at the angle of the central block were first drawn to descend only just below the parapet, and a later line over the old angle shows them to run down to their present level. *Corrections in Thorpe's book*

The subject however is full of difficulties. It is hard to believe that if Thorpe were really the architect of the refined work at Kirby he could also be architect of the much coarser work at Wollaton, except on the supposition that his rough sketches were left to be carried out by Smythson who had a less delicate taste. But Thorpe's own *Difficulty as to Thorpe's position*

[1] *State Papers, Domestic*, Mary, vol. IX. No. 4. Quoted *Transactions of the Roy. Inst. of Brit. Architects*, vol. VI. New Series 1890.

Character
of
Thorpe's
sketches

sketches show none of the refinement of Kirby, the building to which he has the best claim, but abound in Dutch gables, strap-work, and other features of the coarser kind of Elizabethan ornament, of which the only trace at Kirby is in the curved gables of the outer west wall, and in a quite inoffensive way over the drawing-room bay windows. The inner court is quite free from any taint of these extravagancies.

His plan
of Lyveden
new
building

The "new building," as it is called, at LYVEDEN in Northamptonshire is represented in Thorpe's book by a plan which is not signed, but may be assumed to be his from the hand-writing on it. It shows many corrections and alternative suggestions. A staircase in one arm of the plan is struck out, and *buttry all* written across it, another stair in a projecting chamber taking its place. The alter-

Corrections in
nis book

native of a winding stair in another corner is suggested, against which the author writes *or this stairs or porch.* One cannot explain this except on the supposition that the man who made this drawing was the designer of the plan if not of anything further. Whether, if he were John Thorpe, he did more than furnish a ground plan to Sir Thomas Tresham who erected the building, may be doubted, for the "New building" is in a very different style from the generality of the sketches in the book.

Sir
Thomas
Tresham

Lyveden, Rothwell Market House, the triangular Lodge at Rushton, and Rushton Hall itself form a remarkable group of buildings all erected by Sir Thomas Tresham. Rushton Hall is not especially distinguished from the ordinary manor houses of the day, but the other three structures have a very marked character of their own. Sir Thomas Tresham had been brought up as a Protestant, but became an ardent Roman Catholic, and by his buildings he sought to make an everlasting record of his faith in stone. The TRIANGULAR LODGE at RUSHTON which was built between 1593 and 1595 expresses his belief in the Trinity. The three sides are each surmounted by three gables and each contains three windows, which are trefoiled and contain triangular piercings. There are three storeys, and there is a three-sided central pinnacle which also serves as a chimney. The trefoil of the Tresham arms and the motto *tres testimonium dant*, carry on the theme, and each Latin inscription consists of thirty-three letters. The result is a pretty building of banded masonry, picturesque but useless, a freak of orthodoxy and archi- tecture.

Rushton. The Triangular Lodge

LYVEDEN NEW BUILDING (Plate XVII) is also sym- bolical, designed to express Sir Thomas's Christian faith. The plan is a cross with equal arms (Fig. 23) and with a semi-octagonal bay at the end of each arm through one of which is the entrance. The details are very refined, and the mouldings of the cornices very well profiled. English taste and habit fortunately dictated mullions and transoms in the windows, but the rest is quite in the Italian manner. At the first floor is an entablature with a frieze of triglyphs, and in the metopes are the emblems of Christ's passion. The frieze of the upper order contains inscriptions. The building was never finished, nor was the very similar Market-hall which Sir Thomas Tresham built for the neighbouring town of Rothwell in 1577. He was several times imprisoned as a recusant, and two years after his death in 1603 his son Francis died in prison, having been engaged in the Gunpowder Plot, and the estate was then sold to the Cockaynes.

Lyveden new building

Rothwell market-hall

The style of these three buildings is so peculiar that it is natural to suppose Sir Thomas's personality affected

Peculiarity of Sir Thomas Tresham's buildings

the architecture as well as the symbolism. All three,—
even the triangular Lodge in spite of its eccentricity,—
show a degree of refinement, and a knowledge of

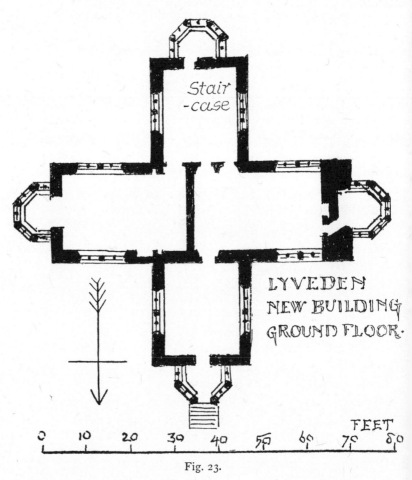

Fig. 23.

good Italian detail superior to most of the contemporary
buildings.

Burghley
House

The great house at BURGHLEY near Stamford, of

Plate XVII

LYVEDEN

Plate XVIII

BURGHLEY HOUSE

Sir William Cecil, Queen Elizabeth's famous minister, has been mentioned already (Plate XVIII). He built three houses; "one in London for necessity, one at Burghley of Competency for the mansion of his Barony, and another at Waltham for his younger son." The last, intended for a "little pile," grew into the vast mansion of Theobalds. The London house on the north side of the Strand, which included what is now Covent Garden in its domain, is described as an enlargement of a house belonging to the Rector of S. Martin's in the Fields, and to have been "a very fayre house, proportionately adorned with four turrets; and curiously bewtified within with rare devices, and especially the oratory placed in the angle of the great chamber[1]." Of Theobalds we have spoken already. Burghley House near Stamford incorporated an older house of Cecil's. He says that "Burghley is of my mother's inheritance who liveth, and is the owner thereof, and I but a farmer. And as for the building there I have set my walls upon the old foundation,...and yet one side remaineth as my father left it me." The house is built round a court, and the east side, incorporating the old house, was finished, with the hall and kitchen, between 1556 and 1564. Further work however seems to have followed with little interruption. In 1570 Sir Thomas Gresham reports that the marble pillars ordered through him have arrived safely from Hamburg. Cecil was created Baron Burghley in 1571 and Knight of the Garter in the year following. As his fortunes prospered and his dignities increased he resolved to make the mansion worthy of his Barony, and erected the three remaining sides of the court, which were built between 1577 and 1587. The date on the great clock-tower (Plate XIX) is 1585.

Marginal notes: Cecil's three houses; The older house at Burghley; Marble from abroad; Completion of the house

[1] Norden's *Middlesex*, cited Charlton's *Burghley*, p. 97.

The plan is finely conceived (Fig. 24).   The greater
length of the court is from east to west.   Entering at the
west end through a vaulted entrance under a turreted
structure you would be faced at the far end of the court

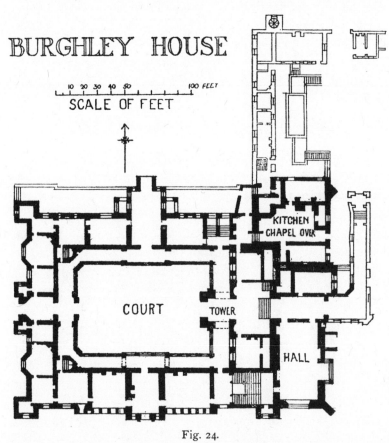

Fig. 24.

by the clock-tower (Plate XIX) with its stone steeple and
ramping supporters, to which the dark cavity of the loggia
on the first floor gives brilliancy and relief.   But the details
of Burghley are unequal to the general conception ; they
have a certain coarseness, as may be seen by comparing

Plate XIX

T. G. J.

BURGHLEY HOUSE

the blunt section of the mullions with that of the graceful
lights of Kirby (Fig. 25) which agree with the section of
a mullion, drawn at the beginning of John Thorpe's book.
There are plans in that book of the ground and first floors
of Burghley, corresponding generally with the actual
building though differing in several particulars. On the
south side Thorpe shows an open loggia on the ground
floor, an Italian idea abandoned as unsuited to our climate.
The space is now thrown into the rooms behind it.

Fig. 25.

The chimneys at Burghley are made like Doric pillars,
an early instance in this country of the idolatry of the
column, and the worship of ancient example. As the
ancients had no chimneys, or at least as they have left us
no example of one, the Neo-Classic felt it necessary to
use such forms as they did leave us, even though foreign to
the purpose. So Scamozzi, whom Chambers supports,
recommends the use of vases or obelisks for chimneys.
The argument is worthy of Nosoponus in Erasmus's
Ciceronianus, who would use no word, nor even any

inflexion of a word which was not to be found in Cicero's writings[1]. In other respects Burghley falls short of the best work of the time. The fantastic pinnacles and cresting on the west front and the curious projection on the north are not happy, and betray a foreign influence. It is known that many Germans, or perhaps Flemings or Dutchmen[2], were employed on the building, so many indeed that, in 1572, Lord Burghley was asked to provide a German church for them in Stamford.

Germans at Burghley

A fine feature of the interior is the stone staircase which has been mentioned already. It consists of two flights returning round a dividing wall: the landings are vaulted with ribs and a pendant, and the two flights with a ramping barrel vault elaborately coffered[3].

The stone vaulted staircase

[1] v. *sup.* Part I. *Italy*, p. 179.

[2] A drawing among the State papers is endorsed in Cecil's handwriting "Henryck's platt of my baye wynd." Paper by Mr Gotch, *Proceedings of the R.I.B.A.* vol. VI. p. 91. New Series 1890. The name seems Dutch rather than German.

[3] Illustrated by a plate from Richardson, in Gotch, *Early Renaissance in England*, p. 187.

EXTRACTS FROM THE BUILDING ACCOUNTS OF WADHAM COLLEGE, OXFORD

The charge from munday the 27 of May till Saturday the 1 of June.

1611

		li.	s.	d.
gs	Ric. Gurden, 12 load ... ... 0 16 0 } xiiij ix x			
	John White, 28 load 1 17 4			
	(& 18 more who are named)			
ſons	For working 12 lights of windows at 3ˢ 4ᵈ ... 2 0 0 }			
ſe	for 50 foote of window Jame at 4ᵈ 0 16 8			
	for working 2 dores at 15ˢ a dore 1 10 0			
	for another dore ... ... 0 6 0 } viij xiiij vij			
	for 53 foote of lodgmt at 4ᵈ 0 17 8			
	for 105 foote of table at 3ᵈ 1 6 3			
	for 456 foote of Aſhler at 1ᵈ 1 18 0			
ʒ	For ridding halfe a qᵃrry at Mag-pit[1] ... 1 0 0			
ne	Chillingworth 51ᵗ & 4 foote of freſtone[2] ... 2 19 10 } v x iiij			
	Smedmore 43ᵗ & 4 foote 2 10 6			
one	Smedmore 80 load of Ragſtone ... ... 1 6 8 } ij viij			
	Chill. 42 load 0 14 0			
s	Wᵐ Arnolls weekely wags ... ... 1 0 0 }			
	Wᵐ Blackshawe, 6 days 0 10 0			
	John Blackshawe, 5 ,, ... 0 7 6 } ij v vj			
	Nath Evans, 6 ,, ... 0 8 0			
ers	Wᵐ Lovis, 6 days ... ... 5 6 } i i			
	(5 more who are named)			
ke	for 8 bars & 12 double lockets[3] for the cellar } 1 13 8 }			
	windows being 10li at 4ᵈ			
	for 300 nayles at 2ˢ 2ᵈ the C ... ... 6 6 } ij xiiij v			
	for 10 hooks for dores weying 51li at 3ᵈ ... 14 3			

N.B. The payments to the men are for labour only.

[1] *Ridding.* Removing the top soil down to the bed of stone. Magdalen College pit.

[2] *Frestone.* Stone for wrought or free-masonry in doors, windows, &c., as opposed to *ragstone*, or *bur*, for backing and rough walling.

[3] *Bars and Lockets.* Bars socketted for passage of one through the other.

		li.	s.	d.			
Boatmen	Wᵐ Howſe for car 16 boat of timber at 2ˢ 1ᵈ				i	xiij	iv

| Lyme | Wᵐ Waker for 8 qᵗʳˢ of brill lyme ... ... | 1 | 16 | 4 | | | |
| | Waltʳ Lerner 4 qᵗᵉʳˢ of lyme ... ... | 0 | 18 | 0 | ij | xiiij | iiij |

| Carriags | Tho Hecks 28ᵗ of timber frō Cumnʳ Wood to the watʳ | 2 | 16 | 0 | ij | xvj | |

| Slats | Edward Triplow for 2500 slats wᵗʰ the carr frō Woodſtocke at at 24ˢ 4ᵈ the M | 3 | 0 | 10 | | | |
| | for 3000 ſlats at 15ˢ the M ... ... | 2 | 5 | 0 | v | v | x |

| Cords | for 2 cords for a Rope ... ... | 0 | 4 | 0 | | iiij | |

| Carigs | for car 3 loads of hurdles[1] 8 load of ſawed timber & 3 load of stayre steps at 10ᵈ the load ... ... | 11 | 8 | | | xj | viij |

Layers	John Loddon & Hugh ffrench for 123 pch of wale at 2ˢ	12	6	0	xij	vi	
	Joseph Row & Ed. Andrewes for 72 pch at 2/-					vij	iiij
	for bottoming a bucket & 2 hoopes for him & 2 for a cowle	1	2			i	ij

	li.	s.	d.
Sū̃m	lxxiij	xiij	ix

161½

From the weekly account March 2ⁿᵈ to 7ᵗʰ.

		li.	s.	d.		
Fremasons to taske	Mʳ Arnold for a bay window for the hall ...	7	0	0		
	for another window for the hall[2]	3	18	0		
	for 189 foote of aſhler		15	9		
	John Spicer for a chapple window[3]	6	0	0	xix	vij
	for 151 foot of aſhler	0	12	7		
	Peter Plomer for a dore		4	0		
	for 144 foot of aſhler		12	5		
	George beale for 51 foot of aſhler		4	3		

[1] *Hurdles* or *Flakes* were used on the scaffolding where we use boards. Hurdles "pro viis supra dictam scaffottam."—*Westminster rolls.*

[2] One of the windows in the *Hall* and *Antechapel* at £3. 18s. 0d. labour only.

[3] One of the windows in the *choir* of the *chapel* at £6. 0s. 0d. labour only.

Blackshawe who had been working as a "fremason" from early in the history of the work was employed to carve the statues over the Hall entrance.

				li.	s.	d.
1612.	Dec. 19.	W. Blackshaw in full paym^t for the chithen[1] vaults		7	10	0
161⅔.	Feb. 6.	W. Blackshaw in pt^e for coping the wall		2	0	0
	Feb. 27.	d^o.	in accompt for the statues	3	0	0
	Mar. 6.	d^o.	d^o.	3	0	0
	,, 13.	d^o.	d^o.	1	0	0
	,, 20.	d^o.	d^o.	2	0	0
	,, 27.	d^o.	for the last of his statuts	3	0	0
1613.	June 21–26.	P^d John Bolton in full accompt for the two skrynes[2] being 82li this being the last payment		9	10	6

[1] *Kitchen.*   [2] The Screens in the Chapel and Hall.

CHAPTER VIII

THE MIDDLE RENAISSANCE (*continued*)

HARDWICK HALL—DECORATIVE PLASTERING— PANELLED DECORATION—KNOLE HOUSE

HARDWICK HALL, "more window than wall," as the old rhyme has it—a very lantern of a house—was begun in 1590 by Elizabeth, Countess of Shrewsbury, a masterful woman, known familiarly as "Bess of Hardwick." She was born in 1520, the daughter of a country squire at Hardwick, but the wealth she accumulated from her three first marriages enabled her to enlarge her modest paternal home into a great house after her fourth marriage with George Talbot the Sixth Earl of Shrewsbury, to whose custody Elizabeth had committed Mary Queen of Scotland. This house—the old Hall—now in ruins, was begun about 1584 and work was still being done on it as late as 1595, when the new Hall, not much more than a stone's-throw away, was nearly finished. The ruins contain many interesting over-mantels in plaster, excellently modelled.

It is doubtful whether Mary was ever at Hardwick; but tradition has it that she was there, and at all events her coming was prepared for, if it is true that the fittings of what is called Queen Mary's room in the new Hall were brought from the old one.

The new Hall (Plate XXI) was not begun till 1590 three years after Mary's execution, when the death of the Earl, the Countess's fourth husband, removed all restraint on her extravagance. He had found it impossible to live with her, and though the Bishop of Coventry wrote to him deploring the separation, he admits that "Some may say in yoᵣ Loʼ behalf that the Countesse is

Bess of Hardwick

The old Hall

Mary Queen of Scots at Hardwick

The new Hall. The Earl of Shrews- bury, d. 1590

Plate XX

KNOLE—CHIMNEY-PIECE IN THE "REYNOLDS ROOM"

Plate XXI

HARDWICK HALL

Plate XXII

T. G. J.

HARDWICK HALL—DECORATED DOOR

a sharpe bitter shrewe, and therefore lieke enough to shorten yo[r] lief if shee should keepe you company....In deede, my good L[o] I have heard some say so[1]." The countess outlived her fourth husband seventeen years, and died in 1607. She lies under a sumptuous tomb which she had erected in her lifetime in Trinity Church, Derby.

Death of the Countess, 1607

The new Hall is a compact symmetrical building, contrasting with the old Hall which was irregular. It is not built round a court, but is a solid block, two rooms in depth, divided by an axial wall, and there are six towers, two on each face, and one at each end. The space between the two lateral towers on each face is filled with a colonnaded Loggia. A hall rising through the ground and first-floor storeys divides the building from front to back in the middle, and the state rooms occupy the second floor above, the whole of one side being devoted to a great gallery. The plan is a new departure from the typical courtyard house of John Thorpe and his school.

The new Hall. Its plan

Novelty of the plan

The Hall seems to have been ready for occupation by the Countess in 1597[2]. It remains very much as she left it. The floors are of beaten plaster on wooden joists ; the chambers and even the staircases are hung with splendid tapestries, and much original furniture remains. The bed-room, called Queen Mary's, is lined with the panelling brought from the old Hall, and occupies the area of one of the towers on the second floor, among the state rooms. In the earlier days of her captivity she was treated with royal ceremony. She had her throne and canopy even after her removal to Fotheringay, for after her condemnation Paulet was ordered to remove it and no longer to

Queen Mary's room

---

[1] Lodge's *Illustrations*, vol. III. No. CCXLV.

[2] v. paper by Mr Stallybrass in *Archaeologia*, vol. LXIV. p. 383, where the history of the two halls is given from the building accounts.

treat her as a sovereign. Her bedroom panelling at Hardwick (Plate XXIII) is handsomely finished and decorated
with painting and gilding : over the door are the royal
arms of Scotland with supporters and the motto IN MY
DEFENS, while round the border of the arch runs the
legend MARIE · STEWART · PAR · LA · GRACE · DE · DIEV · ROYNE ·
DECOSSE · DOVARIERRE · DE · FRANCE~

The panelling is of oak, the styles are stained black,
and the panels, where not covered with devices, are left of
their natural colour. The arabesques are painted in black,
the colour very thin not hiding the grain of the wood.
The arabesques painted on the door bear the date 1599,
showing that fresh work had been put on the wood after
its removal from its original place in the older building.
Similar decoration by painted arabesque occurs on the
door of the state bedroom (Plate XXII). It takes the place
of Italian *intarsia*, such as that at Urbino, and I have not
seen it in any other building. On the second floor the
whole of the east side is given to the great gallery which
runs from end to end of the house. Nearly half of the

The
Presence
Chamber
west side is occupied by a fine room, known as the Presence
Chamber, till lately furnished with throne and canopy,
perhaps in anticipation of a visit from Queen Elizabeth.
There is a good chimney-piece of alabaster and coloured
marble, probably by Accres, or Akers, the marble mason.
The walls are hung with fine tapestry illustrating the
adventures and return of Ulysses[1]. But above is a system of

The plaster
frieze
decoration, very remarkable and indeed unique ; a plaster
frieze at least 9 or 10 feet high, well modelled with forest
scenes, hunting parties of men and dogs, deer, boars and
game of all sorts, in high relief and painted in colour

---

[1] These tapestries are of Flemish make. Two of them have B for Brussels
in the border, and the cypher of the maker Andreas van Dries $\overset{P}{\underset{X}{}}$.

Plate XXIII

HARDWICK HALL—QUEEN MARY'S ROOM

Plate XXIV

HARDWICK HALL—THE PRESENCE CHAMBER

(Plate XXIV). I doubt if there is anything of the kind comparable to it elsewhere.

Modelling in plaster was a recognised form of decora- Plaster decoration tion in buildings of this period. There are many over-mantels of plaster on a large scale in Somerset, at Dunster Castle, Quantoxhead, and the farmhouses round about. Plas Mawr at Conway has ceilings and mural decorations in plaster, and over-mantels with heraldry and badges, dated in 1577 and 1580. Its use in external work and its durability in that position at Nonsuch Palace has been mentioned already. It is used outside on a house at Saffron External Walden, and on many cottages in the Eastern Counties, and plaster work SPARROW'S HOUSE at IPSWICH is magnificent with exterior pargetting (Plate XXV, p. 114). There was a house at Maidstone richly decorated in the same fashion which was destroyed about 1882[1]. Mr Gotch illustrates a cottage at Wivenhoe entirely covered with plaster scroll-work[2]. This device, like that of terra-cotta, if not first introduced into this country by Italians—for in a simple and obvious way, by scraping and stamping, plaster had probably been decorated at all times—was at all events raised by them into a fine art. Their work at Nonsuch perhaps set the fashion, but the English builders readily took it up and developed it in their own way. All great houses in the 16th and 17th centuries had their ceilings of "fret-work," done certainly by Englishmen, for they are quite unlike the stucco work in Italy, or elsewhere abroad. Mr Robinson[3] remarks that had our ceilings resembled those of other countries they would not have excited the admiration of foreign visitors. " The Duke of Wurtemburg who visited England in 1598 expresses himself astonished at their

[1] Illustrated in the *Building News*, Ap. 7, 1882.
[2] Gotch, *op. cit.* plate 117.   [3] *Journal of the Society of Arts*, Ap. 24, 1891.

richness and beauty." The names of many workers in
" Fret " are known. The ceilings of the Library and Com-
bination room at St John's, Cambridge, are by Cobb, who
was paid £30 in 1600 "for frettishinge the gallery and the
great chamber[1]." The ceilings at Knole are by Richard
Dungan, the King's Plasterer, who was paid in 1607 the
balance of £410. 3s. 6d. "for Fretts and other work done at
Knoll[2]." Charles Williams was employed at Longleat, and
as Sir William Cavendish, son of the Countess of Shrewsbury by her second husband, writes to beg the services
of the cunning plasterer, "who had made divers pendants
and flowered the Hall at Longleat[3]," it has been suggested
that he was the artist of the great frieze in the presence
chamber at Hardwick. His name however does not appear
in the list of craftsmen employed at Hardwick given in
Archaeologia, and Mr Stallybrass attributes not only the
frieze work in plaster, but that in stone and alabaster to
Abraham Smith who figures largely in the accounts in
many capacities[4]. The colouring of the frieze was done by
John Paynter or Painter, whose proper name is perhaps
concealed under that of his craft. The long gallery has a
very simple ceiling with moulded ribs which was made by
John Marker[5]. There is another in Queen Mary's room,

[1] Willis and Clark.

[2] I am indebted to Mr C. J. Phillips, F.S.A., for this extract from his collection for his forthcoming work on Knole House.

[3] Mr Robinson's introduction to Millar's Plasterings, plain and decorative.

[4] Archaeologia, as above. Some of Abraham Smith's figures in the chimney-
pieces of the gallery might be taken for Italian work. A marble group of Apollo
and the Muses over one chimney-piece appears from a MS. note-book of the
sixth Duke of Devonshire to have been brought from Chatsworth. This and
another representing the marriage of Tobias do not belong to Hardwick and
are by a superior, probably an Italian hand.

Both Abraham Smith and Accres had been employed by the Countess on
her new house at Chatsworth.

[5] Archaeologia, as above, p. 381.

Plate XXV

SPARROW'S HOUSE—IPSWICH

Plate XXVI

T. G. J.

CEILING AT EAGLE HOUSE, WIMBLEDON

but the absence of fretwork ceilings at Hardwick is remarkable. Even the presence chamber has none, nor even a cornice.

The fretwork plasterer went round the country with his patterns, from which the Employer made his choice. Richard Williams, foreman of the works at Cobham in Kent, writes to Lord Cobham that as soon as the floors were ready " the plasterer would be sent for to come, to bring to y[r] Lo. modells or patternes of the maner of sealing

The fretwork plasterer

Fig. 26.

that y[r] L. maie make yo[r] choice of that kind of work that shall best like yo[u], and some care would be had that he be a good workman and the price reasonable[1]." Even houses of smaller pretension had their fretwork ceilings beautifully modelled and cleverly adapted to irregularities in the room. Fig. 26 shows a simple ceiling at Trent. Coats of arms are often introduced, as in the Gallery at Grove Place,

[1] Paper by Mr Gotch to the Architectural Association, May 12, 1892.

8—2

where they help to fix the date, and identify the builder.
Many of them run riot in strap-work (Fig. 27), an im-
portation from Germany and the Low Countries, a form
of ornament that does much to debase the architecture
in many buildings of Elizabethan and Jacobean date. The
better kind of ceiling consists of ribs, either plainly moulded
as in Fig. 26, or widened out to receive bands of flowers
and fruit. The ribs form various geometrical figures, the
panels between them being either left plain or more

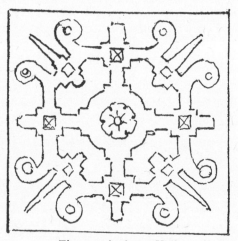

Fig. 27. At Aston Hall.

commonly filled with an ornament, and sometimes with
a figure of man or beast, or with a cartouche and shield
with heraldry. There are four ceilings of this kind, dating
from about 1610, in the house where I write these lines,
where the ribs are prettily filled with floral ornament and
fruit (Plate XXVI). In many cases the ceilings spring from
the walls with a cove, and in others the top of the wall was
decorated with two or three bands of plaster work as at
Haddon Hall (Fig. 28) above the cornice of the panelling,
a device which helps to give height to what otherwise

would seem a low room. There are casts of some excellent fretwork ceilings in the museum at S. Kensington. In later work the enrichments are highly relieved and have a ponderous effect, but the Elizabethan and Jacobean ceilings are in low relief, the ribs rarely projecting more than an inch or an inch and a half, within which distance

Fig. 28.

all the ornament is kept. This kind of ceiling seems peculiarly English, and was remarked and admired by foreigners.

The walls where not covered with decorative plastering were often left with the bare brickwork or stone, which was concealed either by oak panelling, or by arras, tapestry, or in humbler mansions by hangings of say or darnix, that

Panelling is cloth of Tournay. In the panelling there was room for infinite variety of design. The wood was generally very thin, the rails and styles of the framing being less than an inch in thickness, and the panels often only a quarter of an inch. Linen pattern Even those with the well-known linen pattern raised on them need no more than half an inch in thickness. They are

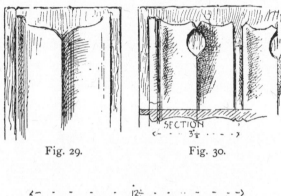

Fig. 29.   Fig. 30.

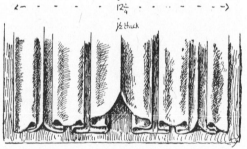

Fig. 31.

Variety of linen panelling formed by running a succession of hollows and ridges along the panel from top to bottom like folds of drapery, and then stopping and shaping the folds at each end in a variety of ways, often very elaborate (Figs. 29 to 33). At Rushton Hall there is a large dining room entirely wainscotted with linen pattern panels. It is a curious invention, suggested perhaps by the linen cloths, *panni*, hung on frames, from

which panelling takes its origin. The device is older than
the Renaissance, and is common in church stalls of the
later Gothic period.

The upper panels are often framed lengthways to re-

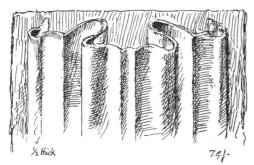

Fig. 32.

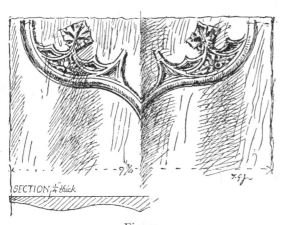

Fig. 33.

ceive a running cornice in carved work. Fig. 34 shows
a panel of this kind at Haddon Hall and Fig. 35 a still
prettier one in an old manor house at Hatfield in Yorkshire.
Chimney-pieces of carved oak panelling abound in all parts
of the country. They have commonly balusters shaped

Wooden chimney-pieces

like Terms at the sides, often with half figures in the upper part, or else there are colonnettes, either single or in pairs, between which are framed enriched panels, generally arcaded and often filled with ornament. The execution is rude, the work of country workmen of little skill, interesting on that account, but more for their simple naiveté

Haddon Hall

Fig. 34.

Hatfield, Yorkshire

Fig. 35.

Birt's Moreton

than for any artistic quality. The room from Birt's Moreton in Worcestershire shown in the illustration (Fig. 36) is a favourable example of a room of this period, decorated with panelling, fretwork ceiling, and carved chimney-piece.

Marble chimney-pieces

In greater houses, the chimney-pieces are of marble very lofty and on a sumptuous scale, carved and gilded

Fig. 36. From *Spring-Gardens Sketch-book*, vol. IV. Plate II.

and inlayed with plaques or bosses of different colours. Some of them perhaps by German or Flemish hands are coarsely designed with strap-work and clumsy scrolls. There is a fine one in good style at Hatfield in King James's room, and those at Knole are superior to most of the kind (Plates XX, p. 110, and XXVII).

KNOLE HOUSE, at Sevenoaks, dates from very early times, but the greater part of what we now see and admire is the work of Sir Thomas Sackville, first Earl of Dorset, poet and author of *Gorboduc* the earliest English tragedy, who succeeded Burghley as High Treasurer of England. In 1566 Elizabeth endowed him with Knole, which he added to his great estate at Buckhurst, like Sir Christopher Hatton who added Kirby to his vast palace at Holdenby. In 1603 he came to reside at Knole and in 1605 began building and enlarging it. Two hundred workmen it is said were constantly employed, and the work went on till the Earl's sudden death at the Council Table in 1608. The building accounts of 1605 and 1606 unfortunately are lost, but the industry of Mr Phillips has discovered some items of expenditure in 1607 and in 1608 the year of Lord Dorset's death. Between August 1607 and the spring of 1608 Thomas Holmden was paid £1489. 8s. 9d. for "defraing of yr Lo building charges at Knole." Richard Dungan, the king's Plasterer, received the balance of his account as I have mentioned already. Halsey and Hawley are paid over £100 for lead at £10. 16s. 0d. the *fettier*; probably a fother, or something under a ton. Kerwin is paid for stone from Oxfordshire and Purbeck. William Portinton the king's carpenter and George White are paid for deal and wainscot, Thomas Mefflyn for glass-work, and Cornelius Cuer, freemason,

Plate XXVII

KNOLE—CHIMNEY-PIECE IN THE CARTOON GALLERY

Plate XXVIII

KNOLE HOUSE—THE CARTOON GALLERY

Plate XXIX

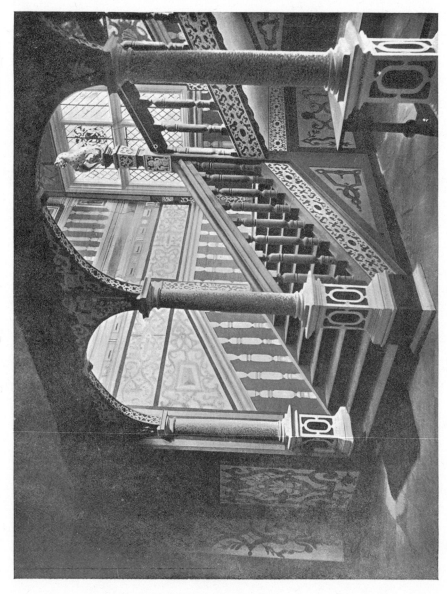

KNOLE HOUSE

for stones for the chimney-piece in the with-drawing chamber[1]. Mr Phillips calculates that during the last three years of his life Lord Dorset spent from £10,000 to £15,000 in building, mainly at Knole.

The staircase of a great house had by this time come to be considered an important architectural feature, no longer to be hidden away in a chamber. That at Knole (Plate XXIX) is finely designed, decorated, and the balustrades and newels are reflected in paint on the opposite wall, as was the fashion in many buildings of the date. At Rothamsted in Hertfordshire there is a staircase with a similar imitation on the wall of the real balustrade opposite. Knole House is built round several courts, and covers a vast extent of ground : I forget how many acres of roof it is said to have. Nowhere are there finer galleries, or more stately apartments (Plate XXVIII), and nowhere else is there a more remarkable collection of old furniture and fittings. The outside has not the ostentation of Wollaton, or Burghley, or Hardwick; the elevation is low, and the architecture simple, for Kent is not a county of free-stone, and the rag-stone of the neighbourhood does not lend itself to detail. The wrought stone dressings had therefore to come from far. But perhaps from its very simplicity Knole has a charm peculiar to itself. There is no other old house like it, and none of which the recollection haunts one more pleasurably. The few architectural details it has are refined and delicate, free from the coarseness that has been noticed in several buildings of the date. Combined with a certain dignity and stateliness there is about Knole an air of true English homeliness that is particularly attractive.

The staircase

Rothamsted

Knole simplicity of the architecture

Its charm

[1] Mr C. J. Phillips, *op. cit.*

CHAPTER IX

THE MIDDLE RENAISSANCE (*continued*)

OXFORD AND CAMBRIDGE—
HALF TIMBER WORK—MONUMENTS

University archi-tecture

THERE is the same air of repose and homeliness about the buildings of our ancient Universities as at Knole, which has always seemed to me to have a collegiate look. Both at Oxford and Cambridge most of the colleges were built or partly rebuilt in the 16th and 17th centuries. They follow more or less exactly the collegiate plan adopted by William of Wykeham at New College in 1379, to which the older colleges conformed when they rebuilt, no less than those that were founded after his time. Stone is the local material at Oxford, and brick for the most part at Cambridge, and both are used with due respect to their natural qualities. The later pre-Reformation colleges, Corpus Christi and Brasenose at Oxford, are in regular Perpendicular Gothic, and so is the Hall and the other work at Christchurch,

Slow pro-gress of the Renais-sance

built by Wolsey for his intended Cardinal College. The new style made its way slowly, and was only adopted grudgingly at both Universities[1]. At first here, as has been noticed generally, the only approach to Classic ex-ample was shown by grafting Roman details on a Gothic

Merton College

design. The tower in the inner quadrangle of Merton has a succession of colonnettes in storey above storey which profess to be Classic, though the rest of the architecture

Wadham College

is in the late Gothic style. WADHAM COLLEGE which was founded the year after this, in 1610, has a similar towered structure over the entrance to the Hall, with four storeys,

[1] See paper by O. Jewitt in *Archaeological Journal*, vol. VIII. pp. 882–96.

Plate XXX

WADHAM COLLEGE, OXFORD

Plate XXXI

THE OLD SCHOOLS, OXFORD

each having coupled columns, Doric on the ground floor Wadham College with a four-centred Tudor arch between them, Ionic in the next with the Founder and Foundress in niches over the arch, Corinthian above with King James I in a central niche, and lastly Composite flanking the royal arms, and surmounted by a curved pediment with quatrefoils and open-work cresting (Plate XXX). The well-known tower Tower of the Old Schools of the five orders in the quadrangle of the Old Schools, now the BODLEIAN LIBRARY, is more ambitious, and though a little later is more Gothic, in spite of its Roman columns (Plate XXXI)[1]. The rest of the Bodleian building shows no tendency towards the new style, but is built in a sober Gothic manner, and the window traceries of Bodley's wing and Selden's are designed fairly correctly in that style (Fig. 37, p. 126). At Wadham however the windows of Hall and Antechapel take a novel form. The lights have very Jacobean tracery flat arches and the head is filled with an oval centre piece flanked by scrolls with plain bosses at the intersections. This design was followed in other colleges, as at University and Oriel. But at Wadham when the builders came to the choir of the chapel (Fig. 38, p. 127) Gothic tradition was too strong for them, and they filled their windows with Perpendicular tracery. These are so correctly designed in Reversion to Gothic at Wadham that style that many antiquaries have refused to believe the two kinds of window shown in Fig. 38 to be contemporaneous and have argued that the Perpendicular choir must be part of the preceding Austin friary. The building

---

[1] The masonry of this tower had decayed, and all the ornamental work including the statues was modelled in Roman cement, which though very hard was coming away from the backing. When repairing this in stone in 1881 I found, on removing the figures of James I, Fame, and the University, that the space was prepared for a window like that facing the street, and that the niches and statues were evidently an afterthought. They were probably put in when the king's visit was expected. Wood says they were gilt, and that the king had them whitened over.

accounts however, show that the Perpendicular windows were actually begun and finished after the Jacobean ones. William Arnold was paid for the last of the eighteen windows of Hall and Antechapel on May 2, 1612, and John Spicer did not receive the last payment for the great east window till September 5th in the same year[1].

East Window.

Fig. 37. From Jewitt.

In other respects collegiate architecture for a long time showed no novelty. The Jacobean quadrangles are entered under a tower with a groined ceiling of lierne or fan-tracery, and the ground-plan follows the quadrangular arrangement of a century and a half before. The college buildings

[1] v. my *History of Wadham College*, p. 46. See above, p. 108, Appendix to chapter VII.

of the 17th century both at Oxford and Cambridge, except Tenacity of the older style for such special features as their purpose required, follow very nearly Dr Boorde's prescription for a private mansion[1].

Wadham College

Fig. 38. From Jewitt.

They have the Hall opposite the gateway, entered from a screened passage with the Hall door on one side and the buttery on the other. The plan is practically that of

[1] v. *sup.* p. 9.

Tenacity of the older style the manor house of the Tudor period such as Sutton (Fig. 9, p. 39) which was followed by those of a later date like Kirby (Fig. 17, p. 69), Knole, Burghley and the rest until the courtyard, a feature inherited from the castle, and having itself a defensive character, gave way to the open plan of Hatfield and Montacute. One may almost imagine that Wykeham's collegiate plan set the fashion not only for academic buildings, but for private mansions of a later

The collegiate plan

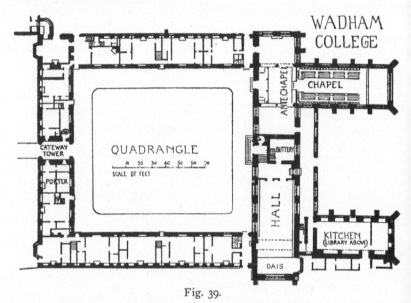

Fig. 39.

date. The two main differences between the plan of such a house as Slaugham Place in John Thorpe's book (Fig. 1, p. 10) and that of WADHAM COLLEGE (Fig. 39) which is the least altered of collegiate buildings, are firstly the necessarily greater importance of the chapel, which in the manor house is often only an oratory, and secondly the The academic library provision of a spacious library.

These libraries at Oxford and Cambridge are veritable

Plate XXXII

MERTON COLLEGE LIBRARY, OXFORD

Plate XXXIII

CLARE COLLEGE, CAMBRIDGE

Temples of the Muses, and to sit and read in them is the very poetry of study. The traditional plan of bookcases standing out at right angles with the wall, forming a succession of pens or pews each with its own window, is the very ideal arrangement for quiet and seclusion, where no sound breaks the silence, but the rustle of the leaves as one turns the page, or the twittering and song of the birds in the umbrageous garden below. Many of them still have fittings of the 17th century, richly carved like those at St John's, Cambridge, or the Reading room at the Bodleian, or the Library at MERTON, which is perhaps the most enchanting of them all. (Plate XXXII.)

The history of the second court at St John's College, Cambridge, is interesting because we have not only the names of the builders, Raf Simons and Gilbert Wigge who began the work in 1599, but a primitive drawing of their design attached to their contract. It is reproduced in fac-simile by Messrs Willis and Clark, and shows how very slight a representation of the work sufficed in those days for a contract[1].

There is no mention of an architect for the beautiful building of CLARE HALL in 1638[2]. (Plate XXXIII.) The builder was John Westley, and a Mr Jackson is mentioned as surveyor, but it is uncertain whether either of them is the author of the very distinctive and masterly design. Thomas Grumbold was paid £3 for a draught of the bridge in 1638, and £6 for working the "Rayle and Ballisters." He also with his sons worked on the building under Westley, and when Westley died in 1644, Robert Grombold succeeded him as master mason. Robert Grombold or Grumbold began the river-front in 1669 in a more

---

[1] Willis and Clark, *Architectural History of the University of Cambridge*, vol. II. p. 256.   [2] Willis and Clark, *op. cit.* vol. I. p. 93.

Clare Hall decidedly Renaissance manner than the older building towards King's College, which in windows and battlements still clings to the mediaeval fashion. In 1684, Robert Grombold is paid 50s. for drawing a design for the north block.

Gonville and Caius College   The gates of Virtue and Honour which have survived that of Humility in the College which was refounded by Dr Caius and bears his name, are very picturesquely designed in a mixed style. The PORTA HONORIS has a four

Porta Honoris centred arch, and other details of a semi-Gothic character (Plate XXXIV). It is said "to have been wrought according to the very form and figure which Dr Caius in his life-time had himself traced out for the architect. It is surmounted by a weather-vane in the form of a serpent and a dove[1]." This pretty structure which has suffered sadly from decay was not finished till after Dr Caius's

Theodore Haveus, his dial death in 1573. Dr Caius's new court contained a column on which was a stone "wrought with wondrous skill containing 60 sundials, the work of Theodore Haveus of Cleves, a skilful artificer, and eminent architect." This has disappeared, but an instrument with a regular dodecahedron is shown in the portrait of Haveus in the College Library. There seems no reason to suppose he was the architect of the building or the architect to whom Dr Caius gave instructions for the gate of Honour[2]. A somewhat similar sun-dial to that of Haveus on a column still stands in the quadrangle of Corpus Christi College, Oxford, and another, which appears in Loggan's print, and in Williams's, once stood on the church-yard wall of St Mary's in the

Kratzer's dials at Oxford High Street. They were both designed by Nicholas Kratzer, Fellow of Corpus, who had been sent to Oxford by Henry VIII to lecture on Astronomy.

[1] Willis and Clark, *op. cit.* vol. I. p. 178.
[2] Willis and Clark, vol. I. p. 172, vol. III. p. 527.

Plate XXXIV

CAIUS COLLEGE, CAMBRIDGE—PORTA HONORIS

Plate XXXV

TRINITY COLLEGE, CAMBRIDGE—THE FOUNTAIN

A still more beautiful structure at Cambridge, standing Trinity College fountain independently like the Porta Honoris, is the FOUNTAIN in the middle of the great court of TRINITY. It is not known who designed it. It was begun in 1602, but was rebuilt in 1715–6, with a few alterations[1] (Plate XXXV). It is an octagon with eight arches on columns, and a delicately carved entablature from which eight ribs spring to the centre with an heraldic lion and shield as a finial. The brattisching between beasts at the angles forms a Brattisching cresting, and being on a small scale is here used legitimately which can hardly be said of that at Wollaton. But it is a form of ornament more suited to wood than stone, and on a large scale it has a very coarse inartistic effect. The screens at the Hall of Trinity College, Cambridge, are full of it and there are many examples of it in the Chapels and Halls of both Universities (Plate XXXVI) as well as in private buildings. Brattisching is akin to the strap-work Its use and abuse that came to us from Germany and the Low Countries, and is only tolerable when treated delicately and not forced into prominence.

Oxford seems to have been rather more tenacious of Oxford more tenacious of Gothic than Cambridge the old style, and less receptive of the new than the sister University. Nevile's Court at Trinity College, Cambridge, (1612) is coeval with the quadrangle of the Old Schools and Bodleian Library at Oxford (1613) but it is less Gothic, and almost as much advanced toward the Renaissance as the garden court of St John's at Oxford which is twenty years later. The Perpendicular Gothic choir of the chapel at Wadham College in Oxford has been described already. In 1620 and 1621 the Hall of Trinity College, Oxford, the chapel of Lincoln College, and that of Jesus were built in a fair Gothic style. The east

[1] Willis and Clark, vol. II. p. 627.

front of Clare Hall of pronounced Renaissance work
was begun in 1638, and was followed at Oxford by
S. Mary's Hall in 1639–40 with windows of regular
Gothic tracery, and in 1642 by the new quadrangle of
Oriel in what may be called the Jacobean Gothic style of
the Bodleian, Wadham College and the Old Schools. In
1630 the great staircase leading to the Hall at Christchurch,
which occupies the interior area of what Wolsey had intended to be a magnificent campanile, but which never
rose above the first stage, was ceiled with a Gothic vault
of fan-tracery springing from a central pillar, by Dean
Samuel Fell, with the help of "one Smith, an artificer
from London."

It would seem from the woodwork in many of the
buildings that have been described that the carpenters
were more susceptible of the new influence than the
masons; for often while the structure itself remained
Gothic the woodwork had quite broken with the school
which gave us the beautiful oak stalls of Gloucester,
St David's, and the royal chapels. The first work in the
style of the Renaissance at Cambridge was the fine screen
of the organ loft in King's College chapel, which as it
bears the arms of Anne Boleyn may be dated between
1531 and 1535[1]. Henceforth we find nothing in woodwork but semi-classic columns and pediments, frets and
guilloches, strap-work and quaint brattischings surmounting
screens in Halls and even in Churches as at Abbey Dore
and at St John's Church in Leeds, a solitary instance of
a church built and handsomely fitted and furnished in
Jacobean times. The Screens by John Bolton in the Hall
and Chapel of WADHAM College (Plate XXXVI) are good
examples of this kind of design, but the most remarkable

[1] Willis and Clark, *op. cit.* vol. III. p. 547.

Plate XXXVI

T. G. J.

WADHAM COLLEGE, OXFORD—THE HALL

Plate XXXVII

CROSCOMBE

From Gotch, *Renaissance Architecture in England* (Batsford & Co.)

is that of CROSCOMBE CHURCH near Wells, where the
screen is surmounted with ornaments rising nearly to the
roof; and the pulpit, which is decorated with painting and
gilding, and the pews are in the same style as the screen
(Plate XXXVII).

The HALF-TIMBERED ARCHITECTURE of England almost
constitutes a style by itself. There is of course plenty of
timbered architecture abroad; the library of the Cathedral
of Noyon was a beautiful example of the 15th century;
I can hardly venture to hope it has survived the late war.
Troyes, Caen, and Lisieux are full of houses of half-
timbered work, and there are examples in the towns on the
Rhine and elsewhere in Germany. But there is nothing
like the rich decorative treatment of Little Moreton Hall,
SPEKE HALL (Plate XL, p. 138), Pitchford, Leominster,
Ledbury, Shrewsbury, and the Feathers Inn at Ludlow.
The principal examples of half-timber are in the West and
North-west of the country. In the South and South-west
of England timber construction is seldom used on a large
scale, but in Surrey and Sussex, where are still patches
of the great Andredsweald that ran for a hundred miles
through those counties into Hampshire, it is very common
in cottages, farmhouses, and to some extent in street
architecture. These buildings are delightfully picturesque,
with overhanging storeys, and recessed bays, between
the two ends (Fig. 40, p. 134). The objection to half-timber
construction is that the woodwork swells and shrinks,
leaving fissures for entrance of water between it and the
plastering, needing constant plugging. It is said that
weather-tiling, so commonly used in the Southern counties,
was invented to avoid the expense of this constant
repair.

Farm-
house at
Wadhurst

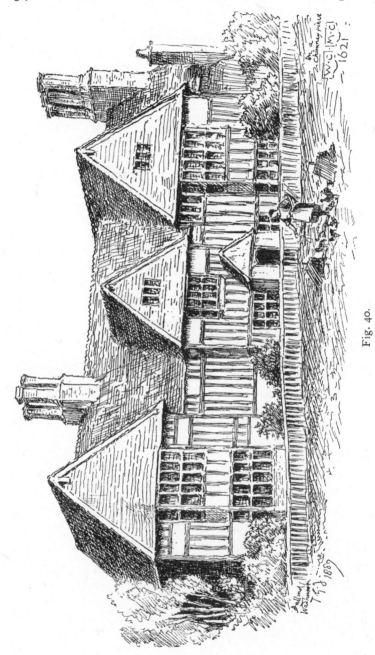

Fig. 40.

Before we take leave of this period of the Early Renaissance something must be said of the tombs which are a remarkable feature in the style. Gothic monumental sculpture in England of the fourteenth and fifteenth centuries had attained a high degree of excellence. The effigies, generally in alabaster, lay on altar tombs with architectural enrichments; often with little figures of weepers, or angels and heraldry, in niches surrounding them. These tombs stood out on the floor and were visible on all sides, and this free-standing position is observed, as I have noticed in a former chapter, in the Italian monuments by Torrigiano of Henry VII, and his mother the Countess of Richmond, at Westminster. With the coming of the Renaissance the tombs were disposed differently. The recumbent attitude was for some time still maintained, but the monument was placed against the wall, and was surmounted by a canopy supported on columns, often running up to a great height, while the back wall under the canopy, either arched or not, was covered with ornament in relief, inscription tablets, and heraldry set in cartouches decorated with colour and gilding. There is a magnificent one of this kind in BREDON CHURCH to Giles Reed and his wife who died in 1611 (Plate XXXVIII)[1]. Westminster Abbey has several; that of Lord Hunsdon, Queen Elizabeth's cousin, being the largest. To bring the figure into better view it was sometimes raised on its side, resting on an elbow, like the figure of General Waller in Bath Abbey, which is of a later date, and of inferior execution, for the skill of the sculptors of the Gothic monuments seems to have expired with the style. Kneeling instead of recumbent figures occur even in the Gothic

[1] The plate only shows part of this monument. There is a good deal of fanciful work above.

period, as in the famous monument of the Cardinal of Amboise at Rouen. In the Elizabethan monuments man and wife often kneel *vis-a-vis* at a lectern, while their children are placed below, boys on one side, girls on the other. The monument of Richard Cecil, father of the Lord Treasurer, in S. Martin's Church at STAMFORD (Plate XXXIX) is a good example of a mural monument of this sort.

Tomb at Stamford

Tombs of Queens Elizabeth and Mary Stewart

The sumptuous canopied tombs of Queen Elizabeth and Queen Mary of Scotland in Westminster Abbey, appear to be executed by foreigners. For that of Elizabeth Maximilian Poutraine[1] or Powtran, alias Colte or Coulte, received £570; Patrick the blacksmith £95, probably for the railing which once surrounded it; John de Critz, or Crites, painter £100; and the whole tomb cost £965[2]. The marbles which are freely used in monuments of this kind are foreign, the black or touch-stone coming probably from Namur in Belgium. There is a fine tomb of this canopied sort to Lord Treasurer Burghley in S. Martin's Church, Stamford. The Paston monument in North Walsham Church, Norfolk, is an elaborate tomb of the

Tomb to Lord Burghley

---

[1] Maximilian Powtran or Poutraine was a native of Arras who came to England at the end of Elizabeth's reign and changed his name to Colte or Coulte. His contract to make the Queen's tomb for £600 is dated in 1604/5. It was finished in 1606. In that year he was commissioned to make the well-known "cradle tomb" of the infant Princess Sophia for £140. In 1608 he was made the King's Master Sculptor, with a salary of £8 and a suit of broadcloth and fur yearly. He was alive in 1641. *Dict. Nat. Biog.*, Lodge's *Illustrations*, vol. III. p. 319.

[2] Charges of the tomb for the late Queene

Maximilian Powtran	Qlxx^{li}	vij^c lxv^{li}
Patrick the blacksmith	iiij^{xx} xv^{li}	besides
John de Crites y^e painter	C^{li}	
Stone wch amounted to	200^{lb}	
	in all	965

Notes and Queries, 3rd series, vol. V. p. 434.

Plate XXXVIII

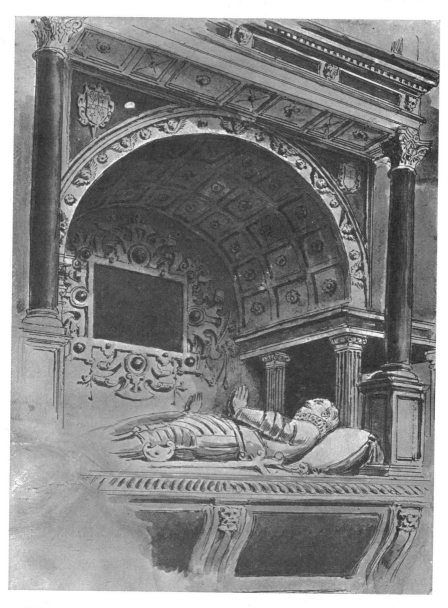

T. G. J.

BREDON CHURCH—TOMB OF GILES REED AND WIFE

Plate XXXIX

T. G. J.

TOMB OF RICHARD CECIL, S. MARTIN'S, STAMFORD

canopied form attached to the wall. A good effect is produced in some cases by chasing a pattern on the polished black marble, and punching or "sparrow-picking"

Fig. 41.

the ground between, leaving the polished surface on the pattern only, which then forms a sort of arabesque in dark on a greyish ground. The tomb of Sir Dudley Digges

Tomb
Chilham

at Chilham in Kent has the black marble columns decorated in this manner; and there are instances of it in many places in chimney-pieces, either on columns, or flat surfaces in pilaster or frieze.

Abundance of Jacobean monuments

The Jacobean period is very rich in sepulchral monuments of this kind, either rising from the floor as those just described, or as mural tablets sometimes containing a bust, like the well-known one of Shakespear at Stratford-on-Avon, or those of Bodley and Savile in Merton College Chapel. There are few churches of any importance without examples of one or other kind of monument, and in many village churches the tomb or mural tablet of Squire or Lord of the Manor is almost the only decorative feature in the building. Akin to these sepulchral tablets are those on almshouses commemorating the founder and his foundation which are often very gracefully designed. Fig. 41 shows one on some almshouses at Maidenhead which were built by "James Smyth Esquior, citizen and Salter of London in yᵉ year of our Lord 1659."

Plate XL

SPEKE HALL

CHAPTER X

REVIEW OF THE EARLY RENAISSANCE

In my first volume which treats of the Renaissance in Italy I described the early stage of the movement, from Brunelleschi to Palladio, as its Golden Age. It was the time when the artists, unfettered as yet by formula and prescription, were still inspired by the tradition of liberty and the reverence for nature which they inherited from the Middle Ages. It was the time of Brunelleschi, Donatello, Ghiberti, Jacopo della Quercia, Michellozzo, Alberti, Rossellino, Benedetto da Majano and Civitale in architecture and sculpture, and of Masaccio, Botticelli, Benozzo Gozzoli, Signorelli, Mantegna and Fra Angelico in painting. The shadow of Vitruvianism and pedantry had not yet fallen on the architect, secluding him in a rigid school of rule and dogma, and setting up a barrier between him and the sister arts. Never was there a time when art was more free, more natural, and more joyous. It had broken through the limitations of the Middle Ages ; it discarded the hieratic restrictions of the Church ; and it went on its way rejoicing in the new powers of achievement which it derived from the example and intelligent study of Ancient Art. Italian art of this Golden Age has a charm that is all its own ; a charm that gradually dwindled away as it fell under the spell of convention and pedantry, till at last it was lost in the cold shadow of an unnatural formality.

During the reigns of Elizabeth and James I, the Renaissance in England was passing through that early stage of its history which corresponds to the Golden Age

of the movement in Italy. Can we say that this period
was the Golden Age of the English Renaissance?

Its freedom   In one respect the conditions were the same. The
art was still free from arbitrary rule; it still enjoyed the
liberty of the preceding age, and even went beyond it,
now and then running into extravagance of novelty with
a spirit to which the somewhat staid and severe style of
Perpendicular Gothic was a stranger.

New social demands on the art   Again it was a rational style. It came at a time when
society was passing into a new phase, and required to be
housed in a different manner. The great mansions of
Holdenby and Kirby, Hardwick and Audley End,
Burghley and Theobalds were devised to satisfy a need
that had never before been contemplated. The mediaeval
castle was out of date; its defences were now useless; its
sombre chambers, massive walls, narrow windows were
unfit for the ease and graces of a peaceful and more civi-
lised way of life. Lodging that had been good enough
for the Lord, was now too poor for the humble retainer.
There had to be great halls and galleries for ostentation,
Superior accom- modation demanded   profuse hospitality, and royal receptions; great windows,
fine facades, terraces and stately gateways; quarters for
numerous guests, and a host of servants. Nor was it only
the great noble who housed himself more luxuriously.
The squire, and the rich citizen, no longer content with
their old quarters rebuilt their houses in town and country,
with bigger rooms, more airy and convenient, and with
better provision for privacy and decency of living: and it
is perhaps in these smaller houses of the Early Renaissance that its charm is most conspicuous.

But while we recognize the influence of the Renaissance on these social changes, by the spread of Humanism,
by the more familiar acquaintance of nobles and gentlemen

with the greater cultivation and refinement of life in Italy, Adaptability of Gothic there was no necessary connexion between these changes and the architecture such as to demand any great revolution in style. There was nothing in the altered domestic habits, and the new way of living to which the native Gothic architecture could not adapt itself fairly well; and in fact it did for some time so adapt itself as to involve little change. The late Tudor houses and palaces such as Sutton and Hampton Court, though planned in the spacious manner demanded by the new fashion, are Gothic buildings: they have mullioned windows, Gothic mouldings, four-centred arches, high gables and turreted gateways, and they have little about them that might not have been done in the reign of Henry VI, except the roundels of Roman Emperors (Fig. 6, p. 28), and the roof pendants (Figs. 7, 8, p. 29) at Hampton Court, and the queer little cherubs in terra-cotta that sportively surmount the doorways at Sutton Place (Fig. 12, p. 42). It is the same at Layer Marney Tower, which is an ordinary Tudor building in the mediaeval style in spite of the flourishing terra-cotta dolphins of the battlements on the turrets (Fig. 3, p. 17).

In the old days these fresh conditions of social life Decay of the Gothic spirit might have spurred the builders to fresh inventions and triumphs in architecture. But things were not now with the Gothic style as they had been two or three hundred years before. Then it seized on any suggestion that led to fresh design. It never stood still but was always changing and adapting itself to novel requirements, and far from clinging to old habits and modes of work it gladly welcomed every opportunity for novelty, every opening for advancing the style to further achievement. Before the Romanesque nave of Peterborough was finished, Hugh of Avalon had built his Early English choir at

Lincoln, and during the following 140 years the style passed to the Geometrical work at Westminster and thence to the flowing Decorated at Ely and Southwell, and lastly to the earliest Perpendicular at Gloucester. Never had the world seen so rapid a progress from style to style, so logical and consistent a development of artistic life[1].

Stagnation of the later Gothic

But there this astonishing effort ceased. It seemed as if the energy that had carried the style ever on and onward had exhausted it; for the next 200 years there was no fresh departure, and the Perpendicular work of Henry VIII in 1530 differs little from that of Abbot Wygeston at Gloucester in 1330 and 1337. And so while everything else was changing architecture stood still. Even had men wearied of it and longed for change, no artistic energy burned within them to evolve anything original: and as the new mode of living made no imperative demand for a revolution in architecture, they were content with the old Perpendicular style which with slight modifications still served well enough. The only great difference was that whereas in the past the great architectural works had been ecclesiastical, in future the art had to deal mainly with domestic and civil buildings.

Survival of Gothic features

The Gothic style succeeded very well in adapting itself with little change to these new subjects. Many ornaments indeed that formed part of the ecclesiastical repertory disappeared as no longer appropriate. There was little occasion for vaulting, except in the oriels of the Hall dais as at Eltham, Hampton Court, and Christchurch Oxford; the windows lost their cusps, and finally the arched heads of their lights, and finished square. But fortunately they

[1] Peterborough Nave was finished in 1193. St Hugh's Choir was begun in 1192, Henry III's Choir at Westminster in 1245, Southwell Chapter House in 1294, the Lady Chapel at Ely in 1321, and the S. Transept at Gloucester in 1330–1337.

House at
Harring-
worth

Fig. 42.

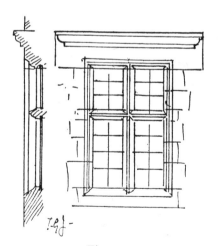

Fig. 43.

kept their mullions and transoms to the last, as in the new building at Lyveden which is otherwise in a tolerably regular Italian style; they appear at LYNDON HALL in Rutland, even after the Gothic style had given way to Classic (Plate XLI), and in houses like that at Harring-

Fig. 44.

worth, which otherwise is built quite in the new manner (Figs. 42, 43). For this we may be thankful: as Anthony Trollope says somewhere no other kind of window gives one so much pleasure, and experience teaches that no other window is so constructional, and in the end so economical in the English climate. Besides this, though the

Plate XLI

LYNDON HALL—RUTLAND

later Gothic churches had lost their high roofs and gables, The high roof which had sunk to a flat pitch and a leaden covering, the steep roofs survived in domestic buildings, not only giving better protection against rain and snow, but affording convenient space for a loft or even an attic storey, with delightfully quaint chambers and picturesque dormers. The The chimney characteristic gable ends and fine clusters of chimney

Fig. 45.

stacks not only of squire's hall but of farm-house and cottage which abound throughout the land are the heritage of the simple rational style of the Middle Ages. Our ancestors of the 16th and 17th centuries delighted in the chimneys, of which Scamozzi and Sir William Chambers were shy because the ancient Romans had left no instructions for designing them. Some of them are constructed, like those made by Robert Burdyes at Hampton

Court, of brick, twisted, moulded, diapered and shaped ingeniously in a variety of ways. There was a singularly

Fig. 46.

beautiful chimney of this kind at EARL SOHAM in Suffolk which is now destroyed (Fig. 44, p. 144). A good effect is produced by grouping eight or ten shafts in one great clump in the middle of the building (Fig. 45). AXMOUTH has a fine example, enriched with chequers of flint and stone and with the builder's initials and date and a pious motto (Fig. 46). The chimneys in Rutland and Northamptonshire are very effective, made of slabs of stone set

Fig. 47.

Fig. 48.

upright and bonded at the corners, with a capital and base to tie them well together (Fig. 47). At Lilford Hall in Northamptonshire the shafts are arranged in a long row, and are connected by arches. Later examples like that from LEWES (Fig. 48) are formed by recesses arched between pilasters of brick. Good traditions secured a proper projection of the caps in due proportion to the shafts.

Survival of
Gothic
In this way the Gothic style, especially in the smaller houses and cottages, went on without more than minor modifications almost to our own day ; and indeed can hardly be said ever to have expired entirely. It was from above and not from within that any change came about, and for some time it affected only the palaces of the great. The Italians imported by Henry VIII, and Francis I, sowed the seed of the Renaissance in both countries, and

Brief
influence
of the
Italians in
England
English carvers, as we have seen, showed no unwillingness to follow the fashion of Italian ornament set them by foreign artists. But the Italians were here too short a time to found a school and inspire English sculpture with a new life. With the departure of Torrigiano and Rovezzano the influence of Italian art came to an end, before it had time to affect the native art of the country.

The
Italians
in France
In France it was different. There too at the end of the 15th century art had sunk into a condition of languor and sterility, from which it was revived by the influence of Il Rosso, and Primaticcio, and the other Italian artists whom Francis I invited and employed. Francesco Primaticcio, says Vasari, came to France in 1531, one year later than Il Rosso[1]. He was sent by Duke Federigo in response to a request of Francis for a man skilful in painting and in stucco. In 1540 the king sent him to Italy to collect marbles, and take casts of the most famous antique statues, from which on his return after the death of Il Rosso in 1541 he cast figures in bronze for the gardens at Fontainebleau. According to one authority he was accompanied by Vignola who remained a short time in France. Vasari says he had helped Primaticcio in taking his casts. The great Lionardo was persuaded to come in 1516, but as

[1] Reveil, *Œuvre de Jean Goujon*, says Primaticcio came first, arriving in 1521, but gives no authority.

has already been said he only came to die. Benvenuto Cellini was in France in 1540, and much courted by Francis who gave him a house, of which he was only able to possess himself by violence[1]. He was employed at Fontainebleau, which he calls Fontana Beliò, and did several works in silver, and made a famous salt-cellar of gold for the king; but he was interfered with by Madame d'Estampes the king's mistress, to whom he had failed to pay his court, and by the rivalry of Primaticcio whom he threatened to murder, and after a stormy career he threw up his commissions, and went home in 1545. Primaticcio however spent the rest of his life in France where he was made Abbot of S. Martin de Troyes, and he died at Paris in 1570. Italian influence therefore in France lasted long enough to awaken the dormant energies of the native artists; and beginning with Jean Goujon, the founder of modern French sculpture, a French school arose of which the traditions are alive to the present day.

England was not so fortunate. The Italians were gone; nothing important in the way of art was done during the short reigns of Edward VI and Mary, and with the accession of Elizabeth who was excommunicated by Rome, and the establishment of Protestantism, intercourse with Italy was interrupted. A new foreign influence came in with the refugees who fled from Holland and Flanders to escape the brutalities of the Spaniards and Alva. The Germans mentioned in the accounts of Lord Burghley's work may have come over for the same reason.

In the Low Countries, as with us, and with the French

---

[1] He had been in France before, in 1537, but was disgusted with his reception and did not stay. "Mi era venuto a noia i Franciosi e la loro Corte, e mi pareva mill' anni di ritornarmene a Roma."

no less, the effect of the Renaissance had so far been superficial. Even later, when the stricter rule of the orders was enforced, the influence of the native art continued to make itself felt. It did so even in France, where the Renaissance was welcomed more readily than with us. " In spite of repeated infiltrations of Italian influence certain national traditions were never lost. The French remained faithful to their large mullioned windows, high dormers, and steep-pitched roofs. Beneath the parade of classical and Italian forms the architecture of de l'Orme, and Lescot, and Bullant, like the poetry of Ronsard and Du Bellay, was French at heart[1]." In Germany too, where the mullion and the high-pitched roof were retained, the native Gothic shows itself even through the Renaissance ornament with which the buildings were often loaded and indeed over-loaded. For German architecture, after adopting the Gothic style from France, instead of persevering in the sturdy native Romanesque of Worms and Maintz, had always tended to extravagance with its immoderately elongated windows, and latterly with bulbous steeples and huge mountainous roofs, of which the grotesque dome over Charlemagne's church at Aix-la-Chapelle is perhaps the worst. And now that the new departure in art seemed to open the door to license the Germans took full advantage of it. Among buildings fairly designed in a sober style are others so belaboured with scrolls, shell and strap-work, broken pediments, vases, and other forms with no relation to nature that all sense of propriety and proportion or of artistic restraint is lost. On such designs as that of the front of the great church at BÜCHEBURG, which was built in 1613, coarse and unmeaning ornament is plastered with lavish profusion and

Survival of native style in France

The Renaissance in Germany

Its extravagance

Church at Bücheburg

[1] Tilley, *The Dawn of the French Renaissance*, p. 456.

Plate XLII

BÜCHEBURG, GERMANY—FACADE OF CHURCH

a hideous result (Plate XLII). Nothing in the wildest Italian *Baroco* ever approached this extravagance; for it never entirely lost the artistic touch.

Still it was from Germany and the Low Countries that much of the ornament of the Early Renaissance in England was derived. It was thence that we got the cut gable, flanked with pinnacles and edged with scroll-work, of Apethorpe and the Western face of Kirby; the strap-work cresting of Wollaton; the chimney-pieces of Bolsover that remind one of a German stove; the cartouches and strap-work ceilings of Aston Hall; and the grotesque Terms that flank the chimney pieces in many a Jacobean mansion. This coarser decoration took the place of what the Italian, had he stayed, might have taught us; and yet through it all a certain British reserve saved us from the extravagance into which the new Teutonic influence might have betrayed us. The simple English gable held its own, and finally expelled the Flemish curved one, the value of plain wall was not forgotten, ornament was economised and used only with restraint, and where it was needed. In all the houses of this date, even in those on a grand scale, there is a certain quiet homeliness that harmonizes with the elms and oaks of the verdant English landscape, and the temper of the English people.

German and Flemish influence in England

British reserve

Its ornament indeed is the weak point of Elizabethan and Jacobean architecture. Comparatively little use is made of sculpture. In that respect it must be confessed the Germans did better, probably owing to their readier access to Italy. In England at this time sculpture was rarely used except on tombs. Many buildings in Germany and the Low Countries were decorated with figure sculpture with good effect; while in England when statues were wanted, as at Audley End, we read of their being

Ornament the weak point in Elizabethan style

imported from Italy. What, we may well ask, had become of the fine English school of sculpture that gave us statues by the hundred on the front of Wells; that carved the angels of Westminster and Lincoln, the storied spandrils of the Chapter House at Salisbury, the delicate figures and foliage of the Lady Chapel at Ely, and many a haunting form or face in stone that dwells fresh on the memory? Were there no successors of the men who carved the

Fig. 49.

lovely trailing foliage of Bishop West's chapel; the capitals at Southwell, so life-like that a cast taken from them might seem to be taken from the plants themselves; of the men who knew by instinct when to imitate and when

to conventionalise, and who could conventionalise without violating relation to nature? These men were gone, and left none to follow them. The British school of sculpture, which was in a languishing state at the end of the 15th century was deadened by the Renaissance, and came round again only to yield to the first bad example that offered itself. Now and then, but very rarely, we find signs of a love of nature, and appreciation of natural form; but for the most part Jacobean carving is unnatural, not even being conventionalised from nature. That shown in Fig. 49 is a fair example of 17th century ornament: the pilaster is carved with rosettes in circles, where an Italian would have placed a graceful arabesque, and the frieze of scrolls and grotesques is a rude version of an Italian design such as that in Fig. 50, coarsened by passing through a Teutonic medium. Decay of English sculpture

It was not only in quality, but in quantity that the

Fig. 50.

deficiency of sculptured decoration was remarkable. I remember a street of comparatively humble houses at YPRES—now alas no more—in which every man had carved on the front some token of his calling or of his fancy (Fig. 51, p. 154). How rare is it to find anything of the kind at this date in England. It would seem that sculpture was a form of natural expression that our people had forgotten. In these houses at Ypres the very cramps that tie them together are made decorative, some of them wrought in graceful scrolls, while others record the date of the building. Houses at Ypres

The need of conforming to the new fashion and of adopting the unfamiliar forms of Renaissance ornament

Houses at
Ypres

Beeste Merkt
Ypres
in 1877 G. Fahre.

Fig. 51.

appears to have paralysed free expression. While Elizabethan and Jacobean architects adopted the columns, entablatures, and conventional ornaments of Roman work, that were paraded before them for imitation, they did not quite know what to do with them. Through them all the old native style asserted itself; in the main all the Early Renaissance buildings in England that we have hitherto considered are really Gothic buildings for all that they are bedizened with Classic orders and for all their pretensions to the new style. And it is in this, and not in their Classic affectation that the charm of these buildings consists. It is this that endears to us the old manor houses and farm-houses of grey stone or mellow brick, with many a gable or clustered chimney stack, in which our country is so rich, in spite of their somewhat clumsy adaptation of alien decoration which the builders did not really understand, nor I think really care for. The quasi-Classic ornaments which fashion forced upon these buildings are not the outcome of healthy natural growth; it is the native art which lies behind it all that keeps them sweet.

Influence of the native style on the Renaissance

CHAPTER XI

THE LATER RENAISSANCE
INIGO JONES AND SIR CHRISTOPHER WREN

The
Vitruvian
style in
EnglandTHE part played by Palladio and Vignola in the history of the Renaissance of Roman architecture in Italy was filled in this country by INIGO JONES. As they reduced the schools of architecture of their time from freedom into obedience to fixed laws and the authority of Vitruvius, so Inigo Jones arrested the eclecticism of the period we have been describing, with a sudden check, and bound the Art fast to Vitruvian canon, and strict Classical orthodoxy. "Towards the end of King James Ist reign," says an anonymous *Critick* quoted in Wren's *Parentalia*, "and in the beginning of his son's, Taste in Architecture made a bold Step from *Italy* to *England* at once, and scarce staid a Moment to visit *France* on the way. From the most profound Ignorance in Architecture, the most consummate Night of Knowledge, *Inigo Jones* started up, a Prodigy of Art, and vied even with his Master *Palladio* himself[1]."

Inigo
Jones,
1573–1653 Inigo Jones was born in 1573, the son of a cloth worker in London, and like his father he was a Roman Catholic. The early promise he showed in drawing and landscape painting recommended him to Herbert, the third Earl of Pembroke, who sent him to Italy. There he studied the ruins of ancient buildings, and worked for some time at Venice, and went thence to Denmark on the invitation of King Christian IV who "first engrossed him to himself." Returning to England he designed the scenes, machines,

---

[1] *Parentalia*, p. 267.

and dress for Ben Jonson's *Masque of Blackness* in 160$\frac{4}{5}$, where he seems to have introduced the novelty and ingenuity of shifting scenery. Masques were the fashion of the day, and the scenery was of greater consequence than the words. As Daniel, for whose masque Jones designed the setting, says, " in these things, wherein the only life consists in show, the art and invention of the Architect gives the greatest grace, and is of most importance." Ben Jonson however did not think so, and he and Jones fell out on the question whose name was to take precedence in the play-bill. Jonson ridiculed him in the *Tale of a Tub*, and in the character of "Coronal Vitruvius," and told Prince Charles that "when he wanted words to express the greatest villain in the world he would call him Inigo."

In 1612, Jones was appointed Surveyor of Works to Henry Prince of Wales at 3s. a day, and was much employed for masques in which the principal nobility, and Royalty itself, played a part. In the following year he was again in Italy, and visited Vicenza, the home of Palladio[1], and also Venice where he met Scamozzi, and resented his depreciation of the great Vicentine master. In 1615 he succeeded Simon Basil as Surveyor General of Works at 8s. a day, £80 a year for "his recompense of availes," and 2s. 8d. a day for riding and travelling charges. His working career lasted till the Civil War put a stop to architecture. He was in Basing House during the siege from 1643 to 1645 and was afterwards imprisoned but got off with a fine. In 1652 he died, unmarried, and was buried with his parents in S. Benet's church, London; but his monument, which was injured in the great fire, finally disappeared when the church was rebuilt by Wren[2].

[1] Palladio had died in 1580.
[2] *Dict. Nat. Biog.*

Inigo Jones was 43 on his return from his second visit to Italy; when he began his career as an architect. He had, it would seem, formed his taste on the lines of Palladio and other great masters of the finished school of the Classic Renaissance, and he came back a convinced Vitruvian.

Lincoln's Inn Chapel
His first public building however, the Chapel of Lincoln's Inn, is Gothic; but he may not have been free to choose his style. In the same year, 1617, he was employed to lay out Lincoln's Inn Fields and began to build the west side, where the gateposts of his work still stand; and in

The Banqueting House, Whitehall
1619, he laid the first stone of the BANQUETING HOUSE, Whitehall (Plate XLIII). Whitehall Palace, which stood across what is now Parliament Street, was created out of York House, the old Palace of the Archbishops, which Henry VIII seized on the fall of Wolsey, and the new building was to replace an old Banqueting house which had been burned down.

Inigo Jones's building is in a pure Palladian style, and might indeed have been built by Palladio, whose work it recalls in many respects. One has to look round at what was being done at that time in England to realize the

Its novelty
impression it must have made. To have a fully developed Vicentine building suddenly dropped down in connexion with the Tudor Palace and Holbein's turreted gateway must have created astonishment and perplexity. Nothing nearly so advanced had yet appeared here. Mansions like Aston Hall and Rushton were rising in different parts of the country in Jacobean Gothic. At Oxford, the chapels of Lincoln and Jesus Colleges, and the Hall of Trinity, in a pronounced though late form of Gothic were not yet begun, and the fan-vault of Christchurch staircase was built eleven years later.

But although Gothic, and the Jacobean form of it still

Plate XLIII

THE BANQUETING HOUSE, WHITEHALL

lingered in the country, and especially at our Universities, the new manner introduced by Inigo Jones made its way at once, and was accepted as the type to be followed by any architect who aspired to be a true disciple of the Renaissance.

For now at last we have the architect in the modern sense fully developed from the transitional stage, of which John Thorpe was an example. Indeed, but for this, it is hard to see how the new art could have made its way so easily, for architecture had now become learned, and needed professors to guide it aright ; and the new style could not be practised in the easy informal way of the Elizabethan and Jacobean schools. It was necessary to understand the orders, and to proportion every feature after the rules laid down by the great masters of the Italian school, based on the gospel according to Vitruvius ; and this demanded higher, or at all events different qualifications from those possessed by the master-mason of the preceding age.

No one can regard the front of the Banqueting House without pleasure : the proportions are well balanced, the details are delicate and refined, and the ornament is chaste and restrained. It is relieved from monotony by the slight projection of the three middle bays which have engaged columns, while the two remaining bays at each end have pilasters, which are coupled with good effect at the corners of the building. The room inside is in one storey of the full height of the building, but the two storeys of the front are justified by the gallery round the interior. Here too we are introduced in full earnest to what, in my first volume on the Renaissance in Italy, I have called the idolatry of the column. The basis of Vitruvian architecture, as understood by Palladio and Vignola and their school is the Order. The Order, as Chambers says, consists of the

Idolatry of the Column

column and the entablature; and there are five orders, differentiated by the five kinds of columns. Classic architecture was in this way focussed on the column, which thus came to be regarded as an indispensable feature in any building pretending to architecture. The great masters of the early Renaissance, Brunelleschi, Michellozzo, Alberti and Benedetto da Majano had no such belief. Vitruvius, though discovered by Poggio in 1414, had luckily not been published in their time, and in the magnificently sane

The Column not abased in the early Italian Renaissance

palaces of the Medici and Strozzi at Florence, and other buildings of the early Renaissance there and elsewhere, columns are only put to their proper use of serving in the construction to carry weight. Roman architecture was studied by these great men sensibly without formula or text-book, and their work is as free as that of the Middle

Vitruvius not a Vitruvian

Ages. Vitruvius himself was by no means a Vitruvian: according to his account of the basilica he built at Fano it would have shocked the Classic Purist. The formulas he gives in his book for the orders apply to Temples, Forums, Basilicas and such-like public buildings for which columnar construction was suitable; for the architectural treatment of private buildings he gives no real instructions. We know now that the Roman house was no more like the Roman temple than our houses are like our churches. But in the 17th century Pompeii had not been excavated, and as the Renaissance architect when he sought to apply

Temple architecture applied to domestic buildings

the lessons of Vitruvius to domestic work found only the prescription for columnar buildings, the column became an essential element in his design for buildings of every kind, whether it were wanted for use or not, and with no reference to its natural function. But Vitruvius is not to blame for that: and San Gallo in the Farnese Palace[1] and

[1] Part I. *Italy*, p. 71, Fig. 4.

Sir Charles Barry by his Reform Club in Pall Mall, have shown us that the abuse of the column is not essential to a fine Classic design.

Inigo Jones however brought back from Vicenza the decorative column, pure and simple, and used it lavishly in all his work. Those in the Banqueting House are useless, supporting nothing, and the entablature has to be broken out without any object but that of covering them. It is a beautiful building, but its beauty is that of a picture rather than of an architectural work. Three cardinal principles should govern all great and living styles of architecture. Firstly, solidity which gives us sound construction; secondly economy, which prescribes proper use of material according to its nature and suitability, and thirdly aesthetic expression of these two conditions of sound building and appropriate design. Here however the main features have no meaning, perform no constructional function, are not suggested by any constructional need, and express nothing. Therefore, I say, that its beauty is pictorial rather than architectural in the highest sense. *The Column as an ornament*

Three cardinal principles of architecture

Pictorial architecture

This criticism cannot be applied to another work of Inigo Jones. In 1631 he was commissioned by the Earl of Bedford to build S. Paul's church in Covent Garden. He was told to be economical; a mere barn would do: and in return he promised it should be the finest barn in Christendom[1]. Here all the architectural features are legitimately employed and a grand and impressive result has been attained with the simplest means. *S. Paul's, Covent Garden*

The Banqueting House was intended for part of a magnificent palace at Whitehall, but it was the only fragment ever erected. The first design, of which drawings by John Webb, Jones's assistant, are in the collection at *Design for Whitehall Palace*

[1] Walpole's *Anecdotes*. He had the story from Speaker Onslow.

Design for Whitehall Palace Worcester College, shows a building 630 feet by 460. The idea was revived by Charles I when he came to the throne, and the size of the building was doubled. This is the design published by Kent in 1727, according to which the palace would have been 1280 feet by 950, reaching from Whitehall Gardens to S. James's Park (Fig. 52). A vast court 800 feet by 400 stretched across it from north to

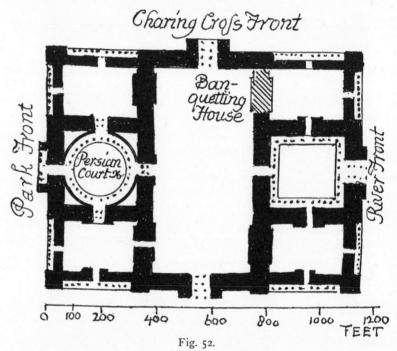

Fig. 52.

south, flanked by a block on each hand containing three smaller courts. One of these included the "Persian" court, which was circular, inspired perhaps by Vignola's circular court at Caprarola[1]. "Persians" stand against the piers on the ground floor, and Caryatides on the storey above. The diameter of this court was to be 210 feet, and

[1] Part I. *Italy*, p. 154, Figs. 19, 20.

Plate XLIV

WHITEHALL PALACE—FRONT TOWARDS WESTMINSTER

Design by Inigo Jones

the whole was on a gigantic scale, the Persians being Design for Whitehall Palace 24 feet high, and the Caryatides 21 feet without the Corinthian capitals they carry. The two storeys together would have been about 80 feet high, and the principal blocks of the palace much higher. Jones has contrived to introduce considerable variety into his elevations, but it may be doubted whether a single building of such vast extent in the same style, covering 24 acres, would not have been wearisome and monotonous. In some of the orders which are rusticated the rustication is carried through the columns by building them with stones alternately round and square, a detestable device. There is a meanness also in the small turrets with cupolas at the central blocks, but a good architect's work is better than his drawings, and in execution Jones might have improved them and made them beautiful (Plate XLIV).

Inigo Jones's design, made pursuant to a Royal Com- Inigo Jones's front to S. Paul's mission in 1631 for rebuilding S. PAUL'S CATHEDRAL which had fallen into decrepitude, was interrupted by the Civil War. But we read that before then he had "put the choir into very good repair, cased great part of the outside with Portland stone, rebuilt the north and south fronts, also the west front with the addition of a very graceful Portico of the Corinthian order built of large Portland stone[1]." The expense so far had been £101,330. 4s. 8d.[2] The Corinthian west front, however unsuitable for the facade of a Norman and Gothic building, is not unpleasing, though the high pitch of the gable required by the nave roof has an odd effect (Fig. 53, p. 164). Fortunately Jones did not try his hand at Gothic, or the result would have been worse, to judge by the attempts of his successor Wren. The same remark applies to his choir screen at

[1] *Parentalia*, pp. 272-3   [2] *Dict. Nat. Biog.*

WINCHESTER CATHEDRAL which was a fine and delicately designed Classic work though obviously inappropriate there

Fig. 53.

(Fig. 54). The screen only remains in fragments but I am able to show a reconstruction from what is left of it[1].

[1] When at work on the Cathedral from 1906 to 1913 I found a great part of Inigo Jones's screen lying in the triforium of the south transept and had the

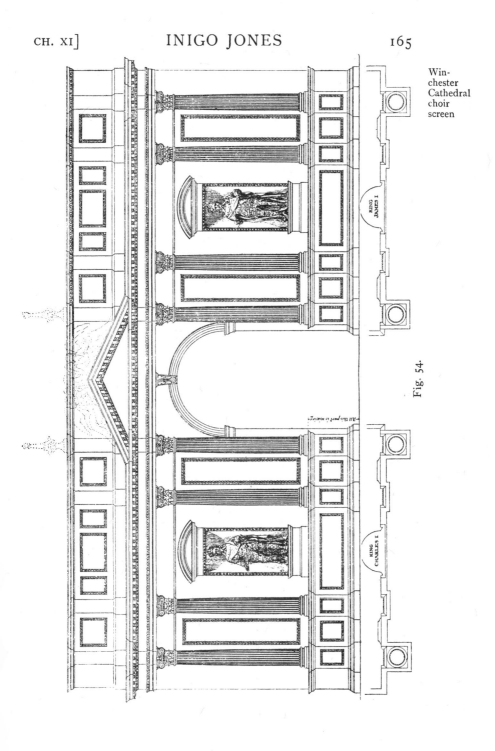

Fig. 54.

Rainham
Park

That Jones sometimes varied his style appears from his design for Rainham Park in Norfolk, where there are curved gables and broken pediments of a Jacobean character. This bears upon the tradition which has always

S. John's,
Oxford

assigned to him the garden court of S. JOHN'S COLLEGE, OXFORD, though there is no evidence for it in the college records or building accounts (Plate XLV). It was begun in 1631 by Laud, then President of the College, and jealous of the two courts at S. John's College, Cambridge, while the Oxford S. John's had but one. The garden front, with its simple lines and graceful though restrained decoration, is well known as one of the most beautiful things in England. This front, and the chambers north and south of the court, are in the usual Jacobean Gothic then in vogue at Oxford, but the east and west faces inside the court are in a florid but irregular Renaissance style, like the famous porch at S. Mary's Church which also has been attributed to Inigo

Nicholas
Stone,
1586–1647

Jones. The latter however is claimed by Nicholas Stone, who built it[1] and says he designed it. In the same way there is a tradition, resting perhaps on no better authority, that Inigo Jones gave Stone the design for the gateway which he built for the Physic Garden at Oxford.

pieces taken down and laid out on the ground. Much of it was missing as the material had been used for a long while in repairing the Cathedral, but enough remained to give the design. The bronze figures of James I and Charles I by Le Sueur are now at the west end of the Cathedral. The central doorway was nearly perfect, and as I happened to be building the Archaeological and Ethnological Museum at Cambridge the Dean and Chapter offered it to the University, and it now forms the doorway between two of the galleries. Many of the stones had Gothic traceries on the back, fragments of old screens used again by Jones inside out.

[1] "The Noble Frontispiece with tuisted Collums hee desined and built att St Mary's Church att Oxford."

Stone's account book written by his nephew Stoakes, and now in the Soane Museum. v. my *History of the Church of S. Mary the Virgin at Oxford*, pp. 127–128.

Plate XLV

S. JOHN'S COLLEGE, OXFORD

Plate XLVI

GREENWICH HOSPITAL.

GREENWICH PALACE (Plate XLVI) is one of the triumphs of the Renaissance. The movement has produced nothing finer either here or elsewhere. It consists of five blocks : two of them front the river and run back to enclose a large court 270 feet wide : two others further back enclose a narrower court, and on the axial line of the two courts but still further back is the Queen's House designed by Inigo Jones for Henrietta Maria (Fig. 55, p. 168).

The old palace of Greenwich, where Elizabeth had been born and had held her court, was pulled down by Charles II after the Restoration, and the first block called King Charles's was begun by Webb from designs left by Inigo Jones ; but the river front was not finished till 1676 by Wren, four years after Webb's death. An asylum for disabled seamen being suggested by Queen Mary with the concurrence of William III, Sir Christopher Wren re- commended the conversion of this unfinished palace to the purpose. He was appointed architect and the work began in 1696. His scheme for using the detached buildings, and drilling them into regular order, is masterly. Taking an axial line from the middle of the Queen's House, parallel to the first block, he built the block called Queen Anne's to correspond with King Charles's, and drew the two southern blocks, known as King William's and Queen Mary's, inwards so that their northern ends presented a front to the river, with a beautifully designed dome on either hand of the opening between them. Hawksmoor, Vanbrugh, Ripley, and Stuart are responsible for the outside elevations, but the grand scheme of the two courts and the buildings facing them with their magnificent colonnades is Wren's, and as I have said there is nothing finer, I might almost say nothing so fine, in the whole range of Neo-Classic architecture.

Greenwich
Palace

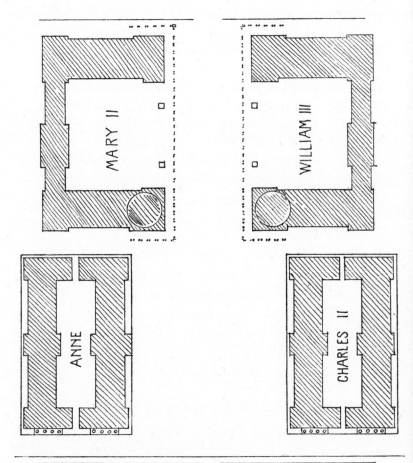

RIVER THAMES

Fig. 55.

Sir Chris-
topher
Wren,
1632–1723

CHRISTOPHER WREN was born in 1632, and was 20 years old at the death of Inigo Jones. On June 25, 1649, at the age of 17 he was admitted a Fellow-Commoner at Wadham College, Oxford, to which he was perhaps attracted by the scientific fame of the Warden Dr Wilkins, who had been instituted by the Parliamentary Commissioners in 1648, to the great advantage of the college. Dr Wilkins though intruded by the Parliament was the Royalist John Evelyn's "deare and excellent friend," whom he even went to hear preach at S. Paul's before the Lord Mayor in the Presbyterian fashion. At Wadham Evelyn saw "that prodigious young Scholar Mr Christopher Wren," who gave him a "piece of white marble which he had stained with a lively red, very deep, as beautiful as if it had been natural[1]." In 1653 Wren was elected a Fellow of All Souls, but he continued to occupy the "Astronomy Chamber" over the gateway at Wadham for which he paid rent in October 1663[2]. He was an original member of what afterwards became the Royal Society, of which the Oxford branch met in Dr Wilkins's rooms at Wadham, Gresham Professor of Astronomy in 1647 and Savilian Professor at Oxford in 1661. Although among the papers he read to the Infant Royal Society at Wadham is one on "*New designs tending to strength convenience and beauty in building*[3]," architecture

[1] Evelyn's *Diary*, July 13th, 1654.

[2] Gardiner, *Registers of Wadham College*, vol. I. p. 178. An indifferent portrait of Wren hangs in the College Hall. On the back is written *Sir Christopher Wren, copied 1825 by Joseph Smith, Oxford, from a picture in the Theatre by Verio, Kneller and Thornhill.* The college has a sugar castor with an inscription recording its gift by *Christophorus Wren, Arm:* in 1653, the year he was elected at All Souls, but though the date mark is missing I was assured by Mr Wilfrid Cripps that the maker's mark proved that it could not have been made till 1720. The original piece was no doubt worn out and the inscription copied on a new one. See my *History of Wadham College*, p. 208.

[3] *Parentalia*, p. 198.

Sir Chris-
topher
Wren

formed no part of Wren's accomplishments till 1663, when he built Pembroke College Chapel at Cambridge for his uncle the Bishop of Ely. The front to the street is simple and not remarkable, but the lantern that crowns it is the best that I know of its kind, and could only have been designed by a born artist. But though his main occupation was scientific, Wren must have shown some capacity for architecture earlier than this, for in 1662 the king tried to induce him to undertake the repair and fortification of the harbour at Tangier, and when he declined the appointment he was made assistant to Sir John Denham the Surveyor General, who Evelyn says was more poet than architect. He was also commissioned to make designs for the Sheldonian Theatre, and additions to Trinity College Oxford. This may have led to his spending six months in France in 1665, where he was introduced to Mansard and Bernini and saw the enormous architectural enterprises of the reign of Louis XIV. On his return in 1666 he was ready with a report on the necessary repair of S. Paul's about which he had been consulted in 1662. After describing the ruinous state of the building and especially the dangerous condition of the central tower, he recommends pulling it down and forming in its place "a spacious Dome, or Rotunda, with a cupola or hemispherical roof; and upon the Cupola—for the outward ornament—a lantern with a spiring top." Remembering the recent theory of "widening refinements" it is interesting to read that Evelyn went to "St Paule's church" where with Dr Wren, Mr Prat, and others including the Bishop of London and the Dean, they "went about to survey the generall decay of that ancient and venerable church.... Finding the main building to recede outwards, it was the opinion of Mr Chichley and Mr Prat that it had been so

His first
archi-
tectural en-
gagements

Wren's
report on
the re-
storation of
S. Paul's

Widening
refine-
ments

built *ab origine*, for an effect in perspective in reguard of the height, but I was with Dr Wren of quite another judgment[1]."

Five days after this visit the Great Fire broke out and the church was burned. Evelyn describes the ruin, and how Inigo Jones's portico—"for structure comparable to any in Europe,—was rent in pieces." Wren reports the same, though he says that "time alone and weather could have no more overthrown it than the naturall rocks, so great and good were the materials, and so skilfully were they lay'd after a true Roman manner." Sancroft the Dean however says the west front was giving way, and that there were two great defects in Inigo Jones's work, that the massy casing of the upper walls rested partly on the groins of the vaulting, and that the new work was not keyed to the old. The idea of repair was finally abandoned, and it was ordered in 1668 that the church should be pulled down and a new one built.

The church burned.

State of the church after the Fire

Wren's first design (Fig. 56, p. 172), which he abandoned with reluctance, and never ceased to regret, is shown by the model which he made at the king's wish, and which still exists in an upper room at S. Paul's. The dome was to be as wide as the present one, 108 feet in diameter; rising however from a *circular* base it had no pendentives and did not challenge the constructional difficulties of S. Sophia, which stands over a *square* of 107 feet. There was to be an outside dome, as at Florence and at Rome, but with a greater elevation above the inner. The effect of the interior would certainly have been magnificent. As you stand under the dome you look down eight converging

Wren's first design for a new church

---

[1] Evelyn's *Diary*, Aug. 27, 1666. See further as to this my *Gothic Architecture in France, England, and Italy*, vol. I. Appendix, p. 289, on "widening refinements."

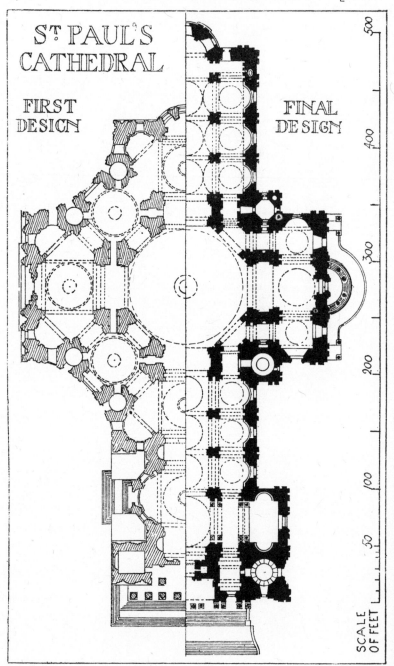

Fig. 56.

vistas, through eight nearly equal arches, and the views The first design
inside the domed spaces round the dome from every point
are surprisingly fine[1]. But the effect of the eight arches,
formed on a curved instead of a flat plane would not have
been good. The plan however did not please the clergy,
who clung to the traditional Cathedral plan, and the dome
certainly is incomparably less beautiful externally than the
one we have.

The design ultimately carried out (Fig. 56) which was The Cathedral plan
begun in 1675 and finished in 1710[2], is based on the
traditional Cruciform English plan of a nave and choir
with aisles and a transept, but over the crossing is the
dome which had been in Wren's thoughts from first to
last (Fig. 56). The area for it is obtained, as in his Area of the dome
uncle's Cathedral at Ely, by expanding the nave to include
the width of the side aisles. On the octagon thus obtained
is raised the drum of the cupola.

In Wren's first and favourite design, of which the plan Advantage of the Greek cross plan
was a Greek cross, the dome would have been well seen
externally from every point of view. In the same way
the dome of S. Peter's at Rome, which is now lost in
the front view owing to Maderno's extension of the nave,
would have been well seen externally had the church been
finished as a Greek cross according to Michel-Angelo's
intention[3].

But in the final plan of S. Paul's the length of the
nave and transepts demanded that the dome should be

[1] All this can be seen inside the model, where there is room for
several persons at once. There is a perspective view taken in the domed
ambulatory in Longman's *Hist. of S. Paul's*, p. 112.

[2] In 1710, "the top stone of the lantern was laid by the Surveyor's Son
Christopher Wren, deputed by his Father, in the Presence of that excellent
Artificer Mr. Strong, his Son, and other *Free and accepted Masons*, chiefly
employed in the execution of the work." *Parentalia*, p. 293.

[3] Part I. *Italy*, pp. 114–120.

raised higher on a lofty drum, if it were to be well seen.

The drum
of the
dome
This drum is surrounded by a gallery with a colonnade as at S. Peter's, but here it is continuous, and every fourth intercolumniation is blocked to form a buttress for the drum. The drum inclines inwards, which adds to its strength, and also to the perspective effect (Fig. 57). The

The inner
dome
inner dome rises to the height of 216 feet from the nave floor, but a glance at the section will show that this was far too low for external effect. Wren therefore raised the

The brick
cone
base of his lantern 50 feet higher on a brick cone, round which is an upper drum carrying the dome of timber and lead which is visible externally. This device has been condemned as a sham: but that might be said of the timber roof over the vault of every Gothic Cathedral. I see no other way in which so good an effect, both external and internal, could have been attained. The inner dome is fully high enough in proportion: some think it too high. To have raised it higher would have converted it into a gigantic and disproportionate lantern. The result of Wren's construction is a triumphant success: from every point of view the dome of S. Paul's is well seen, its outline is perfect, and its beauty is unrivalled. Not less

The
western
towers
successful is the design of the two western towers. To group the comparatively slender proportion of a vertical tower with the swelling outline of a dome is a task to try an architect's ingenuity severely. The minarets that surround so gracefully the domes at Constantinople are too slight to challenge comparison, and they combine harmoniously. San Gallo proposed two lofty towers with a kind of spire at the west end of S. Peter's, as may be seen on the medals of Pope Julius III, but the effect would have been unhappy[1]. Wren by giving his western towers

[1] v. Part I. *Italy*, p. 113.

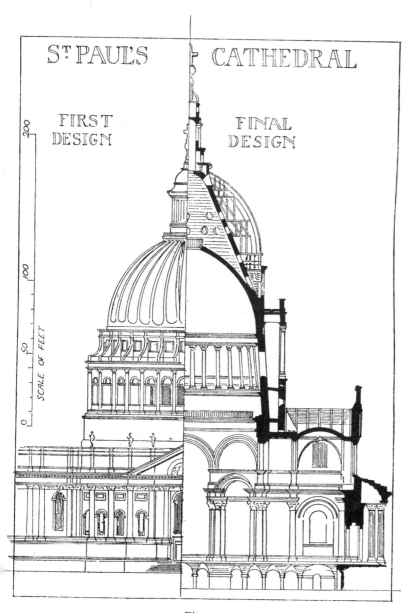

Fig. 57.

a moderate height, and a massive outline by means of re-
ceding stages finishing with a small cupola, has perfectly
succeeded in making his towers not only to harmonize
with the great dome, but to lead up to it and give it
support (Frontispiece). In this and in the numerous spires
with which he has adorned the city he has never been at
fault, and has shown that he had an unerring eye for outline.

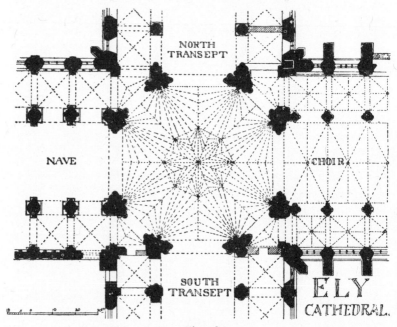

Fig. 58.

Unlike the dome of S. Peter's at Rome, which rests
on four huge piers, the oblique angles of the octagon being
solid, Wren's dome rests on eight piers. At S. Peter's the
piers block the aisles: at S. Paul's the aisles run through
them into the dome area reappearing again on the other
side. Wren's plan is in fact that of the octagon at his
uncle's Cathedral at Ely (Fig. 58). At Florence the

Plate XLVII

TRINITY COLLEGE LIBRARY, CAMBRIDGE

Plate XLVIII

S. MARY-LE-BOW, LONDON

nave aisles pierce the two western piers and run into the octagon in the same way, but they are not continued beyond.

For Wren's brick cone and outer dome there is a Wren's masking sound reason, as I have explained : it is wrong to call it walls a sham. The same defence cannot be maintained for the upper order of the side walls of the body of the church, which have nothing behind them, and are mere screens, hiding the flying buttresses and the clerestory of the nave. Undoubtedly it would have been difficult to have harmonized the narrow nave and low aisles of a Gothic Cathedral with the vast central dome; but though difficult it would not be impossible, and in an earlier style and on a smaller scale it was done by Bramante at S. Maria delle Grazie in Milan. Wren however had not the courage to attempt it, and he has masked the Gothic construction which ecclesiastical pedantry forced upon him by building a screen to hide it. In his first and favourite design his dome is buttressed effectually by eight smaller domed chambers surrounding it, and there would have been no need for any such subterfuge.

It is not possible within the limits of this volume to Sheldonian do more than touch on a few of Wren's works ; on the Theatre Sheldonian Theatre at Oxford with its unsupported timber roof and flat ceiling with a span 70 ft. × 80 ft.; on his splendid LIBRARY at TRINITY COLLEGE, CAMBRIDGE (Plate Trinity XLVII), unrivalled by any building of the kind ; on the College fountain court of Hampton Court ; and on the numerous Library city churches in which he showed not only infinite variety of design, but infinite ingenuity in adapting them to cramped, inconvenient, and irregular sites. One of them, S. Stephen's, Walbrook, just behind the Mansion House, S. has always been admired for the simplicity and beauty of Stephen's, Walbrook

S. Stephen's, Walbrook

the plan. A square surrounded by an aisle is formed into an octagon by throwing oblique arches across the corners, and a dome springs directly from the eight arches of the octagon. One of the fine organ cases for which the churches of this period are famous fills a western gallery, and the plan is produced by an extra bay eastwards. As Mr Penrose has said, "in no other building has so much been made of a plain oblong space and sixteen columns. The secret lies entirely in the arrangement of the plan, and harmony of the proportions[1]."

Wren's steeples

Not less remarkable are the towers and spires of his churches, a feature with which Classic architecture had not hitherto been called upon to deal. A church without a spire would not have satisfied the citizens accustomed to the Gothic churches with steeples and peals of bells which had perished in the flames. The classic campaniles with which Wren adorned London were something quite new, and would have astonished Vitruvius quite as much as the tower and spire of Salisbury. In a few cases, like that of S. Antholin's, now unhappily destroyed, they followed the form of a Gothic broach spire. But generally they consist of a plain lower part carrying several superimposed structures, diminished stage by stage so as to give a good outline. That of Bow CHURCH in CHEAPSIDE is certainly the finest (Plate XLVIII). The spire that crowns the tower of S. Bride's in Fleet Street consists of a telescopic series of similar octagonal structures diminishing as they rise, which might easily have been unhappy, but it will be found that a line from top to bottom touching the cornices of the several stages gives the conical outline which the eye desires, and S. Bride's spire is not the least beautiful of all Wren's campaniles. For outline, as I have

[1] R.I.B.A. *Transactions*, vol. VI. 1890.

said already, Wren had an unerring eye, and infinitely various as his steeples are they are all pleasing. No other country has steeples in the Neo-Classic style at all comparable to them.

One would like to know how Inigo Jones's austere Palladianism would have dealt with the steeple. It was a task better suited to Wren's more versatile genius. The freedom with which he used the forms of Classic architecture, and the liberties he took with the orders have been a provocation to the stricter Classicists. They ask why he dared to group the columns in the front of S. Paul's in pairs, instead of placing them in regular order. They condemn the solid lunettes or tympana of his library at Trinity Cambridge, by which he ingeniously kept the library floor down to a convenient height without unduly depressing the arches and the lower order. They blame the same offence in his fountain court at Hampton, and Fergusson objects to the round windows of the upper storey which nevertheless do more than anything else to give character to the design. Indeed to those who are not wedded to strict Classic orthodoxy it is often the very points with which the Purist finds fault that make the buildings interesting. In all these liberties Wren shows independence of mind and freedom of imagination, not unlike that of the preceding ages of Gothic. The very irregularities of which his critics com- plain give a charm to his style. Imagine the columns in the frontispiece of S. Paul's arranged at equal intervals, and what a dismal and commonplace effect would you have! Alter the fine proportions of Trinity Library and you would ruin the design. These departures from strict Neo-Classic rule, which some attribute to the inexperience of an astronomer set to design architecture without any proper education, will seem to others due to the instinct of an artist free from prejudice, going the straightest way to his purpose, and handling the new style with a freedom that serves to rank him with Michel-Angelo, who was equally contemptuous of precedent in architecture, and of conventional restraints.

It is significant of the age, and of the tyranny of style, that the defence put forward in *Parentalia* for grouping the columns of the facade in pairs is based not on the ground of artistic merit, but on that of ancient precedent for such an arrangement, as if that were of any consequence.

Wren's churches were novelties at that time. Church building, as we have seen, had practically come to an end with the Reformation. Men no longer built churches as a pious sacrifice, or a votive offering, and the country was amply supplied already so far as accommodation was concerned. When therefore most of the churches in London were destroyed by the Great Fire, and new ones had to be built, the question was how to arrange them. The old churches were designed for a form of service that had passed away, and something different seemed desirable. Wren boldly challenged the difficulty : he discarded the mediaeval plan entirely, and started afresh. The type of church which he invented was quite new, nothing exactly like it had ever been done before. The only church at all planned in the same way was the Roman basilica which had galleries, and no structural chancel, the choir being in the apse behind the altar. S. Agnese at Rome without its apse would be something like Wren's pattern for Protestant worship, but there is no reason to suppose he knew anything about the churches of that kind or that date. His churches in plan and

arrangement were based on common sense, regardless of The Protestant plan
precedent, and were adapted to the services of the Reformed religion. He abandoned the distinct chancel: it
would be vain, he said, to build churches in which all the
congregation could not see and hear. For the Romanists,
he says, "it is enough if they hear the murmur of the
Mass and see the Elevation of the Host, but our churches
are to be fitted for auditories." For the same reason he
abandoned the long nave as "impertinent" to our service

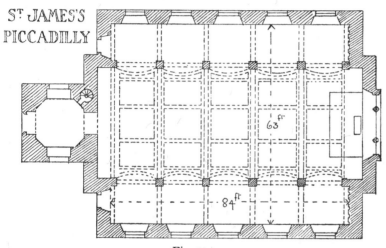

ST JAMES'S PICCADILLY

Fig. 59.

which does not use processions. In S. JAMES'S CHURCH, S. James's, Piccadilly
PICCADILLY (Fig. 59), he considered he had solved most
successfully the problem of seating 2000 people so that
every one could see and hear. His interiors were fitted
with splendid woodwork of oak in galleries, wall-panelling,
pulpits with magnificent testers, and lovely organ-cases.
There were handsome altar pieces, altar rails, finely
sculptured fonts, wainscotted pews, and stately staircases
in spacious vestibules leading to the galleries. Some of the

vestries are models of rich panelling, that of S. LAWRENCE JEWRY, being the most remarkable: it is perhaps the most beautiful room in London (Plate XLIX). The carving of the organ loft and case, and of the doorways in this church is extraordinarily rich and beautiful.

Wren's churches have been hardly dealt with. In some cases futile and absurd attempts have been made to Gothicize them. In most of them the high pews have been cut down, perhaps the most pardonable of the changes that have been made, though it was unpardonable to lower some of the fine pulpits: generally for want of a structural chancel the seats have been rearranged in the Eastern part; worst of all, the windows have been filled with painted glass, mostly bad, but even when tolerable destructive of the intended effect, plunging what was meant to be a cheerful light interior into a miserable gloom and darkness.

Sir Christopher Wren, who had been infamously used by the Commissioners under George I, and was superseded by an incompetent and, as it turned out, a corrupt surveyor of the works, ended his honourable and unselfish life in 1723 in his 91st year. For his work on the cathedral and parish churches he had only asked a salary of £300 a year, and he built the Greenwich Hospital for Queen Mary "without any Salary, Emolument or Reward, preferring in this, as in every other Passage of his Life the publick Service to any private Advantage of his own, by the Acquist of Wealth, of which he had alway a great Contempt[1]."

Wren's master carvers were Grinling Gibbons for wood, and Caius Cibber for stone. Cibber was a native of Holstein. Gibbons, who lived from 1648 to 1720, is

[1] *Parentalia*, p. 328.

Plate XLIX

S. LAWRENCE JEWRY, LONDON—THE VESTRY

claimed by some as a Yorkshireman, son of one Simon
Gibbons who was employed by Inigo Jones ; according
to others he was a Dutchman, and born at Rotterdam,
which however would not necessarily disprove an English
parentage. Evelyn discovered him working in a humble

Fig. 60.

cottage at Deptford, and was so struck with his art that
he introduced him to the King[1] and to Sir Christopher
Wren. He founded under Wren's direction a school of
wood-carvers, many of whom are known by name, and as
it is impossible he could have done a hundredth part of

[1] *Diary*, Jan. 18, 1671.

Grinling
Gibbons the wood carving attributed to him, much of it must have
been by his assistants, and
those who followed his lead.
He has never been sur-
passed in delicacy of carving natural foliage, fruit,
and flowers, but he is of
course well known as a
sculptor of the figure and
larger work as well. His
bronze statue of James II
at Whitehall may rank with
that of Charles I at Charing
Cross.

Ironwork
of the 18th
century The magnificent ironwork of this period must
not be forgotten. For that
at S. Paul's and Hampton
Court Wren employed
Tijou, who is said to have
been a Frenchman, but the
work is very unlike any
French ironwork known to
me, and I think superior.
There are fine gates to the
Temple Gardens, dated
1730; others rather later
to the Clarendon building
in Broad Street, Oxford,
which are illustrated by
Digby Wyatt in his book
on metal work. In Fig. 60
I give a drawing of some

Fig. 61.

gates at Burghley House, which are gilded. But ironwork of fine design and excellent workmanship of this period abounds in all parts of the country. Not less remarkable are the gate-piers to which they are often hung, such as that belonging to a ruined house at Greatworth in Northamptonshire (Fig. 61).

Fig. 62.

Churchyards throughout the country abound in well-designed monuments of the 18th century, both altar tombs and carved headstones. Many of the latter are admirably finished with scrolls of foliage and cherubs' heads, often executed in a masterly way. They are examples of a traditional art which has now expired, and the old-fashioned headstone has lamentably given way to the stone crosses with which our churchyards are made hideous. A fine example of the altar tomb is given in Fig. 62 from the churchyard at IRON ACTON in Gloucestershire, which bears the date 1689. Fig. 63, taken from one in the churchyard

The altar
tomb
at WIMBLEDON, dated 1770, shows a common type, in which the details are well designed in a severer Classic form that could hardly be improved.

Fig. 63.

CHAPTER XII

THE LATER RENAISSANCE (*continued*)

THE work of Inigo Jones had effected a complete Triumph of Roman Renaissance revolution in the practice of Architecture in this country. Thenceforth there was no thought of building anything of importance except in the new style of which he set the example. Gothic, though it lingered in country places, and for some time at the Universities where conservative ideas ruled, gradually changed its character and finally disappeared as a style, though it never ceased in many ways to affect its successor. We may trace its influence Influence of Gothic in the free and genial work of Sir Christopher Wren.

But except in Hawksmoor and to some extent in Gibbs, Wren had no followers. Most of the architects of the 18th century, with the fervour of converts attached themselves desperately to Palladio and the Vitruvians. Wren was slighted by some of them as a very imperfect Stiffening of the new school artist, and the liberties he took with the orders were pronounced heretical. The reversion to strict rule and dogma from the less rigid respect paid to it at first was not complete till the generation that had been contemporary with Wren in the later part of his career had passed away. In the work of Hawksmoor, Vanbrugh, Campbell, and Gibbs we still find individuality alive, not yet crushed out by convention. But these men were all dead by the middle of the century ; Gibbs, the last of them, died in 1754, and with them the first vigour of the Renaissance expired, and its vitality was exhausted.

VANBRUGH, who began an adventurous life as a soldier, Sir John Vanbrugh, 1664–1726 got himself into prison in France for want of a passport, and lay some time in the Bastile, though, as he said, he "had not the slightest idea what had gained him the distinction of detention in such a fortress," and after his liberation he became famous as a wit, and writer of comedy. How he became an architect we do not know, but in 1701, when he was 35 years old, we find him building the great palace of Castle Howard in Yorkshire, for Lord Carlisle. By the influence of the Howards he was made Clarencieux Herald, and would have been Garter, had not the king pointed out the impropriety of appointing a man who had ridiculed the noble science of Arms in one of his Comedies. In 1702 he was appointed Comptroller of the Board of Works in succession to Talman, an architect remembered only by Chatsworth, and by his interference with Wren at Hampton Court. About the same time Vanbrugh appears not only as architect of the Queen's opera-house, but also as lessee, manager, and author, an enterprise by which he lost money. In 1705 he was appointed architect of BLENHEIM, which a grateful nation was to bestow on the Duke of Marlborough. (Plate L.) After the Duke's death in 1722 the Duchess quarrelled with Vanbrugh, finished the building without him, and shut the Park-gates against his wife. He died in 1726.

The well-known epigram, erroneously as it seems attributed to Swift[1],

> Lie heavy on him earth, for he
> Laid many a heavy load on thee

conveys the popular impression produced by Vanbrugh's work. Though it can hardly be called beautiful, it is at all events individual, has character, and therefore commands respect. It is grandiose, ponderous and impressive,

---

[1] It is now attributed to the Rev. Abel Evans, Fellow and Chaplain of S. John's College, Oxford, a protégé of the Duchess, *Dic. Nat. Biog.*

Plate L

BLENHEIM PALACE

Plate LI

QUEEN'S COLLEGE, OXFORD

but suitable only to buildings on a large scale, for when applied to smaller work the result is clumsy and ugly. There used to be a stone house on the site of the present Indian Institute at Oxford, said to have been built by Vanbrugh with material left over from his other buildings, which was an extraordinarily heavy and monstrous piece of work. When dealing with great buildings Vanbrugh's dramatic talent seems to have inspired his architecture. His masses are disposed scenically. On this ground his work appealed to Sir Joshua Reynolds: he says "To speak then of Vanbrugh in the language of a Painter, he had originality of invention, he understood light and shadow, and had great skill in composition. To support his principal object he produced his second and third groups or masses......and no architect took greater care that his work should not appear crude and hard. That is, it did not abruptly start out of the ground without expectation or preparation[1]." Both at Castle Howard and Blenheim (Plate L) there is a great central block, supported by lesser blocks on either hand, connected with the centre by colonnades. Everything of course is symmetrical, for regularity and balance were in the air, as in the contemporary gardening, where

> Grove nods at grove, each alley has a brother,
> And half the platform just reflects the other,

and both at Blenheim and Castle Howard the kitchen in one wing is exactly balanced by the Chapel on the opposite one. The scale of these buildings is immense. Blenheim measures over 800 feet to the extremity of the wings, and the front of the central block alone is 320 feet wide, the length of many a Cathedral.

[1] Thirteenth Discourse, Dec. 11, 1786.

Nicholas
Hawks-
moor,
architect,
1661–1736
HAWKSMOOR, who was born in 1661, is a more interesting architect. At the age of 18 he entered the office of
Sir Christopher Wren as "scholar and domestic clerk,"
and he worked with him for the greater part of his career.
At a later date he helped Vanbrugh at Castle Howard in
1702 and caught some of his grandiose manner. The old
Clarendon
Building,
Oxford
Clarendon Building in the Broad at Oxford is by him,
though perhaps Vanbrugh gave suggestions for it[1]. It is a
building of no great size, but it has a gigantic Doric order,
forming a Portico with columns 3 ft. 10 in. in diameter,
which throws the building, otherwise a respectable piece
of Classic architecture, out of scale with its neighbours.
Hawksmoor's new quadrangle and front to the High
Queen's
College,
Oxford
Street of QUEEN'S COLLEGE at OXFORD is a very stately
and masterly piece of work. In front it has a cloister and a
screen wall with a charmingly picturesque *tempietto* over
the gate; the sides of the court have two storeys above a
rusticated arcade, and the block facing the entrance, containing the Hall and Chapel, is dignified and impressive.
As the interior of this block has only one storey of the
full height of the building, there is very properly a single
order outside from the ground to the cornice. This great
order has been criticized as having an excess of strength,
carrying nothing but a balustrade. But in this style,
attached columns and pilasters were not expected to carry
anything, but were only asked to stand against the wall
and look pretty (Plate LI).
All Souls
College
What could have induced Hawksmoor to try his
hand at Gothic in the north quadrangle of All Souls,
and to produce the most farcical travesty of a style of
which he was totally ignorant, passes imagination. The
College had wanted him to pull down their beautiful

---

[1] £100 was given "to gratify Mr. Hawksmoor," on account of this building.

Gothic quadrangle and rebuild it, but here his good sense saved us from a disaster; he pleaded for the preservation of all the old work that was strong and durable[1]. His scruples however did not prevent him from proposing to pull down the whole of Brasenose College and from de- signing an entirely new building in a heavy Renaissance style, which is illustrated in the *Oxford Almanack* for 1723. It is however far superior to the wretched designs for the same purpose submitted later by Soane and by Hardwick[2].

Brasenose College

Hawksmoor's churches, built between 1711 and 1729, S. Alphege, Greenwich, S. George's, Bloomsbury, and Christ Church, Spitalfields, show both knowledge and originality. The spire of the latter is remarkable for the way in which the lower part is spread laterally, and for its porch carried on coupled columns, with a barrel arched centre. In S. MARY WOOLNOTH, which occupies an awkward site on the narrow fork between Lombard Street and King William Street, Hawksmoor has had a great field for his ingenuity. The south side is quite plain, not intended to be seen, but has been exposed by modern alterations. The other side is without windows, but is decorated with recesses and ornamental details often studied by architects. The west front has a really commanding position facing the widened space where the two streets join, but the contracted site forbad anything like a tower. The church therefore has a frontispiece, shallow from east to west,

Hawks-
moor's
churches

S. Mary
Woolnoth

[1] There is a dreadful design in William's *Oxonia* for a new mock-Gothic front to All Souls, and a plan for reconstructing the whole College. In the same work are plans of a similar kind for dealing with Magdalen. There seems to have been a mania at that time for altering the whole aspect of the University.

[2] All these designs are illustrated in a paper I contributed to the *Magazine of Art*, for Aug. 1889.

spread out to the north and south, with a rusticated
lower storey, finishing above in a pair of small turrets
with a pierced parapet between them (Plate LII).   In

Hawks-
moor's in-
dividuality
all these churches Hawksmoor has shown strong individuality : they are entirely his own, unlike anything by
his contemporaries, and are free from slavish subservience
to the strict dogmas of Palladianism.   He is described as
an amiable unassuming man, " well known for the even-
ness of his temper, which was not disturbed even by the
most poignant pains of the gout.   He was perfectly skilled
in the history of Architecture, a good mathematician, a
scholar of languages and an excellent draughtsman[1]."   He
died in 1736.

James
Gibbs,
architect,
1682–1754
Of the group of early 18th century architects mentioned above, GIBBS in his work most resembles Wren,
and comes nearest to him in merit.   James Gibbs was
born in 1682, the son of a merchant in Aberdeen.   He
was helped by the Earl of Mar to travel in Italy, where
he studied under the younger Fontana, and after his return
in 1700 he began practice as an architect.   His first im-

S. Mary-
le-Strand
portant work was the church of S. MARY-LE-STRAND,
which was built between 1714 and 1723.   It was one of
fifty new churches ordered by an Act of 1708 under
Queen Anne, and as this was in an important place Gibbs
says the Commissioners "spared no cost to beautify it."
The church was to have had only a small bell-tower, and
at some distance westward was to have been a lofty column
with a statue of the Queen.   But Queen Anne died before
this column was begun, and Gibbs was told to substitute
for it a steeple to his church.   As this was already half
built, and as a width from east to west of only 14 feet
was provided for the small bell-tower, the only thing to

---

[1] *Dict. Nat. Biog.*

Plate LII

S. MARY, WOOLNOTH, LONDON

From the *Builder*

Plate LIII

S. MARY-LE-STRAND, LONDON

be done was to expand the steeple sideways and make it S. Mary-le-Strand oblong. This Gibbs managed very successfully, so far as the east and west faces were concerned, by adding detached columns on the north and south sides, and keeping pilasters on the east and west faces. The tower therefore is oblong, and the north and south sides are very narrow. But those sides could hardly be seen on account of the narrowness of the streets, and it was not till the new streets on the North were opened in our day that the leanness of the side aspect was exposed. The completion of the building scheme now in progress to the North may perhaps once more mask it. (Plate LIII.)

The church is small and has no aisles, but is made to look larger by the two orders which give it scale, and the tower and steeple are certainly among the most beautiful in London. Like Wren, Gibbs had a good eye for outline, and he has not been less successful at S. Clement S. Clement Danes Danes, where in 1719 he finished the steeple which Wren had left incomplete.

The church of S. Martin-in-the-Fields which Gibbs S. Martin-in-the-Fields began in 1721 is more important. In plan it follows the model originated by Wren, of a quadrangular building with nave, side aisles, and galleries, and without distinct chancel. The interior, now plunged in dismal and oppressive gloom by the painted glass with which the windows have unhappily been filled, is simple and dignified. Gibbs however has crowned his columns with an entablature block of the full proportion of the order, a The entablature block device employed by Brunelleschi at Florence in the churches of S. Lorenzo and S. Spirito, and by the Romans in the Baths of Diocletian, and elsewhere. It is a piece of pedantry : the order is supposed to be incomplete with a column only ; it must have its entablature, and if the column is isolated it must have a bit of the entablature on it returned four-square. This is of course an improper use of the entablature which is a feature of trabeation, to be used as a lintel between two supports, or as a cornice running along a wall. If something of a pedestal on the top of the column were wanted to stilt the arch, it should have been specially designed for the purpose, not made out of a feature designed for a different use. Such special devices occur sometimes in Italian Gothic, as for instance at Siena Cathedral where they are well managed. Wren has done much better at S. James's, Piccadilly, where he runs regular entablatures from the columns back to the outer wall of the church, and turns a waggon vault from one to the other; and at S. Bride's he has a short entablature on coupled columns, as in S. Costanza at Rome, which is a perfectly legitimate use of it[1]. Fergusson, who also objects to this entablature block, makes the amusing suggestion that it would be better to turn it upside down on the capital, in which position it certainly would be equally sensible.

The outside of S. Martin is more interesting than the inside. The portico with its grand flight of steps is a fine feature, the tower and steeple are magnificent and nothing could be more happy than its position at the top of Trafalgar Square.

In 1722 Gibbs began the Senate House at Cambridge, which was to have been followed by two similar blocks, which were never built, forming three sides of a quadrangle, and in the next year he designed the new building
of KING'S COLLEGE, which has the air and grandeur of a Roman palace. It is a very stately and dignified piece of

[1] v. Part I. *Italy*, pp. 56–57.

Plate LIV

KING'S COLLEGE, CAMBRIDGE

Plate LV

THE RADCLIFFE LIBRARY, OXFORD

work. Two storeys of plain wall with well proportioned King's College, Cambridge windows rise above a rusticated ground storey; there are no idle columns or pilasters, and there is only a cornice without frieze or architrave. In the middle is a grand archway under a pediment carried on columns. Nothing in this way could be better. (Plate LIV.) The same Gibbs's domestic work restraint is shown in Gibbs's domestic work, as at Ditchley in Oxfordshire and Catton Hall in Derbyshire.

Hawksmoor had been consulted about the building at King's College, and had made a design and model for it, but the scheme fell through before Gibbs was consulted. He also made a design for the RADCLIFFE LIBRARY at OXFORD The Radcliffe Library, Oxford which was unsuccessful, and Gibbs was appointed architect. Dr Radcliffe, who had been Court physician to William III, and was famous for his wit, the brusqueness with which he treated his patients from Royalty downwards, and the accuracy with which he predicted their death, died as he had himself foretold in 1714. Besides many bequests to his College and University, he left £40,000 to the University for the purpose of building this library, with money for endowment and purchase of books. The square in which it stands, bounded by S. Mary's Church, the Bodleian Library, and All Souls and Brasenose Colleges, was then covered with small buildings and old schools, which had to be acquired and demolished. Gibbs in his *Bibliotheca Radcliviana*, published in 1747, gives plans, "uprights," sections, and ornaments of the building with Portraits of Dr Radcliffe and himself. "Mr *William Townsend* of *Oxford*, and Mr *William Smith* of *Warwick* were employed to be Masons; Mr *John Phillipps* to be the Carpenter and Joiner; Mr *George Devall* to be Plumber; Mr *Townsend* Junior to be Stone-carver; Mr *Lind* of *Long Acre London* to be Carver in

Wood; Mr *Artari* an *Italian* to be their Plaisterer in the Fret work Way; Mr *Michael Rysbrack* to be Sculptor, to cut the Doctor's figure in marble, and Mr *Blockley* to be Locksmith." The first stone was laid on June 16, 1737 "*Plaudente undique Togata Gente*," and the building was finished in 1747.

This building, so conspicuous in every view of Oxford that it is not easy to imagine Oxford without it, seems to be the one of which Gibbs was most proud, and it is a magnificent memorial both of him, and of the Founder. The Library consists of a domed chamber with a diameter of 48 feet, surrounded by a lower aisle making the extreme internal diameter 88 ft. 6 in. The height inside the room is 60 feet to the springing of the semi-circular Dome. There is a vaulted basement below this, and the height from the ground to the top of the lantern scales in Gibbs's section about 140 feet. The basement, vaulted in stone, once open, but now enclosed by glass to contain books, is rusticated and finishes with a simple cornice without frieze or architrave. Above is a Corinthian order of attached columns with an entablature and parapet surmounted by vases. The columns are coupled, and have between each pair windows and niches alternately. From the eight solid bays containing the niches arches are thrown with grand sweeping buttresses above them to the drum of the dome. The roofs and the dome are of timber covered with lead. A fine geometrical stair in an oval compartment leads to the Library, and smaller newel stairs mount to the gallery of the Library and the terrace over it[1].

---

[1] The Taynton stone used in the building has not stood so well as the hard bed of Headington used for the exterior buttresses. Many of the urns on the parapet had been replaced by terra-cotta which had split to pieces. In the recent repairs I had the pleasure of renewing them in hard Clipsham stone.

The
Radcliffe
Library,
Oxford

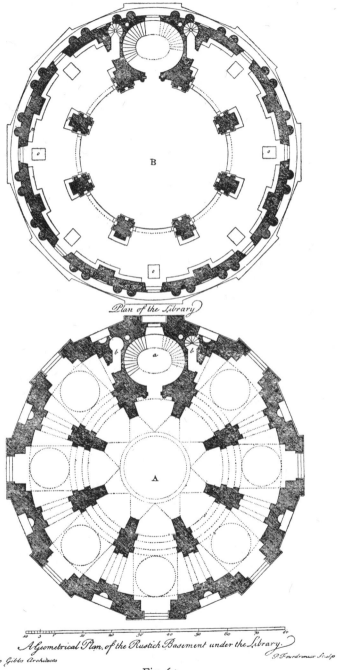

Plan of the Library

A Geometrical Plan of the Rustick Basement under the Library.

Jacobo Gibbs Architecto   P. Fourdrinier Sculp

Fig. 64.

Radcliffe
Library

The fret work done by "Signior Artari, an excellent artist" as Gibbs calls him, is not very interesting. He seems to have been employed by Gibbs very largely. His work is of a florid *rococo* character when it goes beyond mere patterns of rosettes or guilloches.

Revolution
in domestic
architec-
ture

Domestic architecture in plan as well as in style, had now undergone a change as great as that which Wren had introduced into ecclesiastic buildings. His churches do not differ from those of the Middle Ages more than the houses of the end of the 17th and the 18th century from those of the Early Renaissance. The courtyard type of

The
courtyard
abandoned

Audley End, Knole, and Rushton, survivals of the mediaeval Castle with its baileys, and of the defensible mansion, had been given up except at the Universities, where we still build Colleges round quadrangles in spite of the disapproval of Dr Caius at Cambridge and Sir Christopher Wren at Oxford. Already in Elizabeth's time Montacute and Wollaton had abandoned the courtyard for a simple block of building; and Hatfield and Aston Hall at the opening of the 17th century were built with the fourth side of the court open. The great houses we have just been describing, and those on the same or nearly the same scale by Campbell, Flitcroft, and others

Imitation
of Palladio

during the 18th century are all planned in the new manner, generally based on Palladio, and the plans and elevations of many of them will be found in his book. Mereworth in Kent and Lord Burlington's villa at Chiswick are examples of this. The plan of KEDDLESTONE HALL (Fig. 65), by Adam, is copied almost identically from a design by Palladio for a villa on the Brenta[1]. Everything had to yield to ostentation and display to which interior convenience if necessary must give way.

[1] Illustrated in Ware's edition of *Palladio*, Lib. II. Plate LVIII.

Plate LVI

RADCLIFFE LIBRARY, OXFORD (Section)

There had to be a central block containing a hall and the Keddle-
stone
Hall principal rooms, with a subordinate block at a little dis-tance on either hand, containing the offices in one and the stables in the other, which were joined to the central block by corridors either curved or straight. All this of course was suitable only for the palaces of grandees; the style had now to be adapted to lesser habitations: and nowhere was

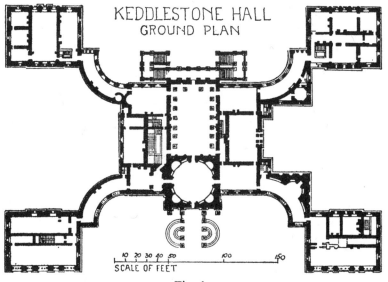

KEDDLESTONE HALL
GROUND PLAN

SCALE OF FEET

Fig. 65.

there a more inviting field for experiment on a large scale than at Bath.

BATH, a small, closely packed, and rather squalid little Bath and
the Woods city at the opening of the 18th century, was brought into notice by the visit of Queen Anne and her Consort to drink the waters in 1702 and 1703, and became fashion-able. The rush of visitors was so great that the villages round about were filled with them, and rooms were let for a guinea a night. A building era set in, and we read

Bath

that in twenty years spent in improving the private buildings of the city "thatched coverings were exchanged for
such as were tiled; low and obscure lights were turned
into elegant sash windows, as soon as Mr Taylor,—who
was by the way a chairman,—had set the example ; the
houses were raised to five and more storeys in height,
and every one was lavish in ornaments to adorn the out-
sides of them in profuseness[1]." The opportunity was
seized in 1724 by John Wood an architect in Yorkshire,
who says : "I began to turn my thoughts towards the
improvement of the city by building, and for this purpose
I procured a plan of the town which was sent me into
Yorkshire in the summer of 1725, where I at my leisure
hours, formed one design for the ground at the north-west
corner of the city, and another for the land on the
north-east side of the town and river[2]." The two John
Woods, father and son, practically re-created Bath and
gave it its distinguishing character.

John
Wood,
Senior,
1704–1754

This system of laying out streets and squares with
houses contiguous and alike was something new. It was
perhaps introduced by Inigo Jones, when he formed the
Piazza, or *Place* of Covent Garden for the Earl of Bedford
in 1633. Hitherto each man had chosen his site and built
his house to his own fancy. Now the houses were built
wholesale on speculation and let on lease, or sold subject
to restrictions. The type of house adopted by Wood had
perhaps been imported in the time of William III from

Uni-
formity in
street ar-
chitecture

---

[1] Wood's *Description of Bath*, p. 225, cited in *The Eighteenth Century
Architecture of Bath*, M. A. Green, p. 13. Mr Green says sashed windows
were introduced at Bath about 1696. Webb had put them in at the Vyne in
1654, see above p. 47. Sashes were put into the Provost's Lodge at Eton
in 1689–1690, and Dr Bentley sashed the Master's house at Trinity College,
Cambridge in 1700, Willis and Clark, vol. III. p. 556.

[2] Green, *op. cit.* p. 34.

Holland, where we find the typical London house, with offices in a basement, a hall and dining room on the ground floor and a study behind, a front and back drawing room on the first floor, and bedrooms above. On no other plan can so much accommodation be squeezed into the same area. Queen's Square was Wood's first work; the houses are strongly built, and well-finished with good staircases and spacious rooms, some of them handsomely panelled. No. 15 on the west side where Wood himself was living in 1730 is even magnificent within, though not distinguished from the rest outside. It has a splendid staircase carved and moulded in Spanish mahogany, and niches and panels of plaster work with figures and ornaments round the landing[1]. The middle house, No. 24, in the north front to which Wood moved, and where he died in 1754, is scarcely less handsomely finished inside. A house at the north-east corner of the Square, with a round end is extremely cleverly planned. The younger Wood lived in it. The Circus was begun by the elder Wood in 1754, the year of his death; the Crescent is by his son. In the former the sweep of the enriched cornice has a fine effect, and the columns are confined to each storey; but there are too many of them, two between every pair of windows on all three floors. In the Crescent one order of columns runs through two upper storeys. The houses in the streets of this quarter of the town, which was laid out by Wood, are built in a substantial sober style, dignified and simple, and this character runs through the whole city, where till modern times there was no intrusion of gaudy vulgarity.

[1] Mr Green thinks the plaster enrichments are by the brothers Francini, Italians who were employed in S. Mary's Chapel in Queen's Square, which is now destroyed. The obelisk in the middle of the Square, was the gift of Beau Nash in 1738, *op. cit.* pp. 59, 63, etc.

The same restraint, and the same correctness of detail is observable in several country houses round about Bath, and indeed throughout the country at this period. Certain standards of taste were accepted as paramount: they were based on the books of Palladio, Vignola, Serlio, Perrault The architect's text-books and others, of which there was a great number either written in English or translated from Italian and French; and these were the text-books not only of architects but of all superior craftsmen. In the list of subscribers to Kent's volume with the designs of Inigo Jones, published in 1727, are the names not only of noblemen and prelates, and of architects like "Colen Campbell Esq., Nicholas Hawks- Their use by crafts- men moor Esq., and James Gibbs Esq.," but those of "Mr Thomas Churchill *Bricklayer*, Mr Christopher Cass *Mason*, Mr Rob. Hodson *Cabinet-maker*, Mr Thomas Howard *Carpenter*, Mr John Hughes *Plaisterer*, Mr John Lane *Joyner*, Mr Bartholomew Peisly *Mason* at Oxford, Mr James Richards *Carver*, and Mr William Sykes *Painter*," and many more such. Some of these operatives were even themselves authors of short treatises Craftsmen as authors on the orders according to Palladio for the use of their fellow craftsmen[1]. Following these books, with plates of the orders and all the proportions in modules and minutes Vignola the workman could not go far amiss. As Vignola says: "all the proportions are founded on simple numbers, you need not trouble yourselves about feet or inches, but only the module and its parts ; so that any man of mediocre intelligence, and with something of a taste for art, may easily master this otherwise difficult subject[2]." Architec-

---

[1] I picked up at a book stall such a book by George Jameson Carver dated 1765, Edinburgh. The subscribers to it are mostly Masons and Joiners. The frontispiece shows the author at work with mallet and chisel in his working dress.

[2] He writes of "La distribuzione delle proporzioni fondata in numeri

ture was thus brought within the reach of any man of ordinary wits, and though his work might be purely mechanical it could not at all events fall into the grosser forms of bad taste as long as he followed his text-books. In this way the traditions of correct proportions and details were firmly implanted in the minds of the craftsmen, who were capable of carrying out in a correct style general instructions given by the architect. So much was this the case that Wren thought it necessary to explain and almost to apologise for sending detail drawings to his men. It was indeed much as it had been in the Middle Ages, when the craftsmen knew exactly how to execute the details of a design ; with this difference however, that the Gothic architect was the master-mason, living at the work, and working manually himself, whereas in the 18th century the Architect was a Gentleman, living and working in an office away from the building.

Architecture, thus brought, as Vignola says, to the level of mediocrity became attractive to the *dilettante*, and many amateur architects entered the field. At Oxford Dean Aldrich is credited with the designs of Trinity College Chapel, All Saints Church, and the Peckwater quadrangle of Christ Church : Dr Clark designed the Christ Church Library, and at Cambridge Sir James Burrough, master of Caius College, Italianized several of the buildings. In all these works it is important to distinguish how much of the design is due to the amateur. Every artist will admit that an accomplished amateur

semplici, senza havere a fare con braccia, ne piedi, ne palmi di qualsivoglia luogo, ma solo da una misura arbitraria detta Modulo ; divisa in quelle parti che ad Ordine per Ordine al suo luogo si potrà vedere, e data tal facilità a questa parte d' Architettura altrimente difficile, ch' ogni mediocre ingegno, purchè habbi alquanto di gusto dell' Arte, potrà in un' occhiata sola, senza gran fastidio di leggere, comprendere il tutto, ed opportunamente servirsene."

[Marginal notes: Tradition among craftsmen; Tradition in the Middle Ages; Architecture and mediocrity; The amateur architect]

Amateur helpless in detail

will often make valuable suggestions, and even form general conceptions of a design, which may be worked out with success. But this working out is impossible without the knowledge and experience of an expert who has given his life to study of the art. Aldrich, perhaps the most accomplished of the amateurs I have mentioned, no doubt gave the general idea of the beautiful steeple of All Saints, but he is supposed to have had the advice of Wren, and the draughtsmanship of Hawksmoor; and Burrough, of whom it is said "his works are certainly not characterized by great artistic power, and are all in the tamest Italian style," had the help of Essex, an architect who made designs also for Corpus Christi College of which one of the Fellows pretended to be the author[1].

Lord Burlington

Lord Burlington is the most distinguished of the amateurs. A smattering of architecture had now become a fashionable accomplishment, though one ought not to know too much, and Lord Chesterfield says Lord Burlington had "lessened himself" by too profound an acquaintance with details. He is probably entitled to more credit for the designs published under his name than is allowed by Sir R. Blomfield[2], but he had the help of Kent who, after his return from Italy in 1719, actually lived in Lord Burlington's house till his death in 1748. Kent's design for the Horse-Guards' building in Whitehall is excellent in its way. It has fortunately escaped the additional storey by which one Prime Minister thought to improve it[3]. The traditions of Inigo Jones, Wren, and Gibbs were carried on respectably, if not with any striking display of genius, by their successors during the 18th century, till the

William Kent, 1685-1748

The Horse-Guards

---

[1] Willis and Clark, *op. cit.* vol. I. p. 298, vol. III. p. 536, etc.
[2] *Hist. of the Renaissance in England*, vol. II. p. 223, etc.
[3] I believe it was once proposed to put a similar top storey on Wren's Library at Trinity College, Cambridge, one of the master-pieces of the world.

severity of the school was invaded by an outbreak of eclecticism and finally of revolt. There was Ware, the *Ware* architect of Chesterfield House, and Editor of Palladio; there was Flitcroft who built S. Giles-in-the-Fields with *Flitcroft* a good steeple in the manner of Gibbs, and designed the great houses of Wentworth and Woburn; and Campbell *Campbell* who compiled the *Vitruvius Britannicus*, built Wanstead House, and Stourhead, and claimed to be the real architect of Lord Burlington's semi-circular arcade in Piccadilly. There were the two Dances, of whom the elder built the *The* *Dances* Mansion House, and designed the not quite successful steeple of S. Leonard's, Shoreditch, and the younger who built that grim prison of Newgate, stern and forbidding, over the door of which might have been written the words *di colore oscuro* that Dante read over the Gate of Hell, and who showed us that a blank wall may be the finest thing in architecture.

Hitherto the strict regime of Palladio and Vignola had been undisputed, and so far from showing any signs of relaxation, the tyranny of style had been enforced with *Tyranny* *of style* greater severity than in the earlier and more genial days of the movement. Architecture, no longer a field for imagination and free artistic conception, had become a matter of scholarship and orthodoxy, of obedience to prescription and formula. Against this the modern European *Revolt* *against* mind was certain to revolt sooner or later. In all intel- *Palla-* *dianism* lectual fields the rule of authority and dogma was beginning to be questioned. In Italy the strict rule of Palladianism was submitted to for barely two generations after the death of Palladio, and then architecture broke loose, and plunged into the licence of the *Baroco*. In England the revolt took a saner form, more in keeping with our national reserve. The work of the Adams, though ostensibly Classical was none the less subversive of the stricter rule. Men began to find Palladian architecture too costly for common use, and to complain of the expense of the lengthy colonnades and the great portico which formed an indispensable ornament of every design, but was purely ostentatious, always useless, and sometimes inconvenient. They grew tired of sacrificing internal arrangement to outward display, of planning symmetrically and scenically with balanced masses rather than with a view to domestic economy, and they began to ask whether architecture need be inconsistent with comfort and moderate expense.

Here the Adams came to the rescue to some extent in the matter of decoration. Their flat pilasters with ornaments of stucco, and their chimney-pieces with wreaths and scrolls of whitening and glue, their dainty plaster ceilings of delicate modelling, which were all well executed and have stood the test of time, were no doubt a relief from the more solid and monumental work of their severer predecessors, and they have about them a kind of feminine prettiness that is not unattractive. The day of the "Grand manner" was declining: men were looking about for a change; other styles were beginning to challenge the Roman: the publication of Stuart's

Athens, of which the first volume appeared in 1762, created a *furore* for Greek architecture which had the worst consequences imaginable. If, as Fergusson very well puts it, Palladio had undertaken a "task that no human ingenuity could successfully perform, in trying to adapt the Temple architecture of an extinct civilization to the Ecclesiastical, the Municipal and Domestic architectures of his own time," what hope was there of successfully adapting the style of an age still more remote, and

still more alien to our age and our civilization. That The Greek revival
Palladio failed, Fergusson continues, "is not to be wondered at ; on the contrary he deserves all praise for the
extent to which he did succeed[1]." The attempted Neo-
Greek revival however, so far from having any success at
all, has given us the dullest and most frigid buildings of
modern times.

The last man of note belonging to the old school of Sir William Chambers, R.A., 1726–1796
the Roman Renaissance was SIR WILLIAM CHAMBERS.
Brought up for a mercantile career he went to China, and
was fascinated by the architecture of that country, to
which we owe the pagoda he afterwards built in Kew
Gardens. In 1744, at the age of 18, he began to study
architecture; and when George III to whom, when Prince
of Wales, he had been appointed architectural tutor, came
to the throne, Chambers was made Royal Architect,
Comptroller of the Office of Works, and Surveyor
General. His *Treatise on Architecture*, splendidly printed
and illustrated, was published in 1759, and is still recognized as a text-book. "By his influence with the King he
was mainly instrumental in bringing about the formation
of the Royal Academy in 1768, and his business-like
ability served to steer it successfully through its early
difficulties[2]." Among his many buildings Somerset House Somerset House
is that by which he will chiefly be remembered. It
occupies the site of the old palace of Protector Somerset,
which was pulled down in 1775, and the new building, to
contain government offices, was begun in the year following. The river front is magnificent, and is certainly one
of the finest things in London ; though those who can
remember it before the lower part of the terrace, originally

[1] *History of Modern Architecture*, vol. I. pp. 155–156.
[2] Hodgson and Eaton, *The Royal Academy and its Members*, p. 46, etc.

washed by the river, was buried in the Embankment, recognize this curtailment of its primal dignity. The whole design is restrained, and nothing can be better than the open colonnades of the centre, and the two wings. The Strand front is narrow and less interesting, but the entrance with its triple passage and coupled columns is worthy of comparison with that of the Farnese palace.

But Greek and Chinese architectures were not the only rivals with which the Roman Renaissance had to The Gothic revival contend. During the whole period of the Renaissance our native Gothic art had never been forgotten, and its influence had coloured the whole of the new style. Wren himself is represented by his grandson as averse from it, and yet he voluntarily chose to work in that style on more than one occasion. His Gothic work is no doubt amateurish, and shows entire ignorance of detail, but the Wren's Gothic tower of S. Michael's, Cornhill, and the crown steeple of S. Dunstan-in-the-East, of which he was especially proud, have a true Gothic air in their general effect, and Tom-tower at Oxford, though the details are coarse, and out of scale with the delicate 16th century work below, is finely conceived, and the outline might well have been James Essex and Gothic projected by a Gothic master. James Essex, though he built much at Cambridge in the Italian style, was an ardent admirer of mediaeval architecture. He studied it at Ely and King's College, and in 1775 read a paper to the Antiquarian Society on Gothic architecture, which he said had once " adorned this kingdom with many Elegant Structures." He even collected materials for a history of Gothic architecture which fell through for want of sup- The Romantic movement port[1]. The growing regard for mediaevalism was part of the Romantic movement which began in England and

[1] Willis and Clark, *op. cit.* voi. III. p. 543.

Plate LVII

SOMERSET HOUSE, LONDON

spread rapidly through the Continent. There was a re- The Romantic movement
vulsion in Literature from the school of Pope to that of
Thomson, Goldsmith, Gray, and Collins ; a revolt in fact
from convention and a return to nature. The cold regularity of the Classical school was abandoned for the
warmer expression of human sympathy and pathos, and
a passion awoke for the mysterious and supernatural. To
this temper the Middle Ages appealed strongly. Mac- Romance in Literature
pherson's *Ossian*, and Chatterton's forgeries fanned the
flame, more legitimately fed by Percy's *Reliques of Ancient
Poetry* in 1765, which fired the enthusiasm of the boy who
was to become the Arch-priest of Romance[1]. Horace
Walpole's *Castle of Otranto* in 1764 began the series of
romantic novels with a supernatural element, which was
continued by Mrs Radcliffe, and the younger Beckford at
the end of the century.

The romance with which the Middle Ages, and all Romance and Me-diaevalism
that belonged to them were invested in those days was
of course fictitious. Carlyle says somewhere that no age
was ever really romantic to itself : that Orlando probably
had short commons, hard beef to chew, and suffered in-
digestion like ourselves. But in the days of Horace
Walpole less was known about the coarse realities of
those times, their barbarous features were softened by
perspective ; the quaintness of the old writings was
seductive, the ruined abbeys and broken castles of me-
diaevalism touched the chord of sentiment, they seemed
wrapped in mystery and appealed irresistibly to the
imagination, and the revival of Gothic architecture took
its place as part of the Romantic movement. In 1747

---

[1] "I forgot the hour of dinner, notwithstanding the sharp stimulus of
thirteen, was sought for with anxiety, and found still entranced in my
intellectual banquet." *Autobiography* in Lockhart's *Life of Scott.*

210 THE LATER RENAISSANCE [CH. XII

Horace
Walpole,
1717–1797
Horace Walpole bought Strawberry Hill, and in 1750 he writes " I am going to build a little Gothic Castle." It resulted in an inconvenient plan, with its tiny Cloister, Prior's Garden, and dreadful chimney-pieces designed by Mr Bentley, or copied from the Confessor's Shrine at Westminster with improvements by Mr Adam. His Gothic and that of Font Hill Abbey have become notorious and proverbial. There was nothing really Gothic about them, for Gothic architecture is not a matter of pointed arches, quatrefoils and trefoils, pinnacles and traceries as was then supposed, but of a certain sincerity in construction of which all these features are but accidents. This however is how the Gothic revival began; it was promoted on equally imaginary grounds by the High Church party, to whom everything mediaeval was sacred, and it was long before the style was really understood.

But we have brought the history of the Renaissance of Roman architecture in England to an end, and to pursue the story further would be foreign to our purpose.

CHAPTER XIII

CONCLUSION

THE history of the Renaissance of Roman architecture in England has now been traced from the beginning under Henry VIII to the time of its decline, when it had to contend with rivalry and revolt. In order to understand its permanent effect on English art let us consider what the Renaissance really amounted to.

It was a movement, as I observed in my first volume on the Renaissance in Italy, unlike anything that had ever happened in the history of art[1]. Till it appeared architecture had progressed steadily from one phase to the next by imperceptible steps, each being the natural sequence of that before it. There was no break in its advance : it was the same art from first to last, changing from infancy to adolescence. Into this the Renaissance broke violently from without. It was the interruption of an existing vernacular style ; the introduction of alien forms and principles of design into a living and popular art which was being practised with satisfaction. Nothing like this, the abandonment of a living style, and the adoption of one that had been dead for centuries, had ever happened before.

Except at Florence, where it began, the new art was not at first welcomed even in Italy. The Venetians, who adopted it grudgingly, after a brief experience, found the stern Palladian regime cold and unsympathetic ; and early broke away into the license of the *Baroco*: at

[1] v. Part I. *Italy*, p. 24.

Bologna men left instructions in their wills that their monuments should be in the old fashion, *more antiquo*; at Milan a mixed style prevailed, and the building of the Duomo in the Gothic manner went on without interruption; but nevertheless Neo-Classic art triumphed throughout the country before the end of the century.

Triumph of the Renaissance

Its slow acceptance in England In England the tenacity of the Gothic style was still greater. But here as in Italy the revival of Classic scholarship led naturally to the study of Roman architecture, and it became necessary to be in the Classic fashion in building as well as in letters. The Italian artists introduced by Henry VIII and Wolsey led the way, and though they departed on the death of their patron they sowed the seed of the revolution in style that followed.

Adoption of Classic details Endeavouring to follow their example men took the pillars and entablatures of the Romans,—Doric, Ionic, Corinthian, and the rest,—and applied them to the only kind of building they knew; and the work of the early Renaissance is really nothing else but Gothic bedizened with trimmings of Classic architecture, which had no effect on construction or general design. The result was only to create confusion. Confusion of styles The Classic details had lost their meaning: they were used in ways for which they were not intended: it is not in them that the charm of Kirby and Longleat, Knole and Hardwick consists; we look through them to the staple Gothic work upon which they are only grafted as accidental features.

Inigo Jones Then came Inigo Jones, who had studied Vitruvius and Palladio at the fountain head, and had mastered the mystery of the Module. He first showed the English how the Italians had systematized the style. He taught his countrymen that the features they had ignorantly been playing with were part of an ordered scheme based on rules of which they had no conception, and that Roman The grammar of architecture architecture had to be learned like a language with a strict grammar that must not be violated. The lesson was learned, and from that time architecture became subject to rule and dogma, obedient to antique example, and the text-books of Italian masters.

This was the end of the old native traditional liberty. Rule of dogma established Authority and precedent took the place of direct appeal to Nature: the flow of imagination was checked, and men for the first time began to think in styles. Architecture was stiffened into uniformity; ornament that had been free and natural was confined within bounds; for the infinite variety Limitation of forms of the Gothic capital there were but four Roman types and no more from which to make your choice; for decorative features there were the column and entablature, and these had to be used in the same proportion whether on a large scale or a small one; for your chimneys, having no Classic example you could use Doric pillars, urns, or obelisks; for your facade, you took the columns and pediment of the front of a Roman temple,—its head detached from the body—and set it up over your front door. Thus we get the everlasting portico of Blenheim, Prior Park, Wanstead, The Portico Keddlestone, and hundreds of "gentlemen's seats," and of every public building of importance in this style. It was even thought necessary to add one to the back of the old Gothic house of The Vyne in Hampshire to give it a more fashionable air.

The essential principle of the Renaissance was the The style fixed establishment of a fixed style. Styles there had been in Gothic, but they were not fixed: on the contrary they welcomed change and invited development. The Renaissance on the other hand insisted on definite immutable rules, and regular proportions based on ancient example.

It formulated in fact a grammar of design, and by way of vocabulary gave us certain unalterable forms and features which like the words in a sentence you could arrange and combine within definite limits but must not vary.

Contrast
with
liberty of
Gothic
This was of course a complete revolution in European architecture. Not that Gothic had been without a system. It had its own rules and traditions, so general that buildings at one end of the kingdom differed very little from those at the other; and when the style changed, as for instance at Gloucester in the 14th century, the change spread at once to the ends of the country. But these rules were not so much rules as habits, easily changed with the times as the times themselves changed. For every one of these changes grew naturally out of the existing practice; they were not imported from without but were simply improvements, legitimately developed from what was being done at the time. Any artist who had a new idea was free to give it expression, and if it were a good one it spread rapidly from his workshop to the ends of the land. There was no Gothic Vitruvius and no Gothic Palladio or Vignola to check it.

Stagnation
the result
of Palla-
dianism
By the system of the Renaissance on the contrary the style was fixed and all further development arrested. It may be doubted whether Palladio or Vignola imagined that by their new grammar they were bringing the course of architecture to a standstill for ever. They may have thought they were merely rescuing the art from confusion and putting it once more on the right road. But the effect of what they did was stagnation. The great men at the beginning of the Renaissance, indeed, were not enslaved to the letter of the style; the steeples of Wren and Gibbs are after all more Gothic than Palladian. But their lesser followers despised originality and were content to work by the

text-books. As Vignola says, with the help of his treatise Architecture, otherwise so difficult, was brought within the reach of any man of middling intelligence and a little taste for Art[1]; and the later work of the style bears more and more evidently the stamp of mediocrity, far removed from the grandeur and refinement of Whitehall and Greenwich, the library at Trinity College, Cambridge, and other master-pieces with which the movement began.

It is scarcely necessary to say that this stagnation of architecture is inconsistent with the ideas that govern modern life, which is restless, changeful, always demanding novelty and progress. It could not last, and as we have seen, it yielded to strange adventures in art. So long as it did last the stiff rules of the Palladian school saved us from excesses of bad taste. Text-books were in every-body's hands, whether professional or amateur, traditions grew up among the craftsmen, and within those limits they could not go far wrong. So long as the spell lasted, though architecture became tame and commonplace, it did not become vulgar.

Then the spell was dissolved and throughout the greater part of the 19th century the battle ranged between Gothic and Classic. It was not so much a battle of principles as of styles, for the Gothic revival inherited the dogmatism of the Classic revival, and the tyranny of style was in-sisted upon by pedants on one side as much as on the other. The strict Gothic school therefore failed like its predecessor.

The result has been the chaotic condition of Archi- tecture at the present day. Traditions of art there are

[1] Ch' ogni mediocre ingegno, purchè habbi alquanto di gusto dell' arte, potrà in un' occhiata sola, senza gran fastidio di leggere, comprendere il tutto, ed opportunamente servirsene.

v. Part I. of this work, *Italy*, p. 184.

End of tradition

none; they have all been destroyed by successive revolutions. It stands to reason that any Renaissance of a forgotten art *must* destroy existing traditions. Gothic traditions perished before the Roman Renaissance, which to some extent replaced them by others. Then came the Gothic Renaissance which swept these all away, and never succeeded in establishing others in their place except to some extent in Church building. Now there is none, and without tradition, which is a very different thing from style, art is at a loose end.

Discussion on modern art

We have lately been told "it seems to be generally admitted that there is something wrong with the arts. Are we moving on? Are we only treading a wearisome circle? Or have we reached the final bankruptcy of Art[1]?" The mere fact that we ask this question; the mere fact that we discuss in the newspapers the state of our art, or even the want of it, is perhaps the most hopeless sign of the situation.

Its futility

Art is not a matter of talking but of doing. To live, it must be natural, spontaneous. It must come to our conception as naturally as our language to our lips; it must be the free expression of our ideas, unfettered by formal rules, and unchecked by premeditation. It must flow from us unconsciously. To talk about it means that we regard it

Self-consciousness fatal to art

consciously, and for art to be self-conscious is fatal. To bring it into the field of conscious effort is to kill it. No man was ever made a better artist by reading about it in the public prints, or by listening to the critics, any more than anyone was ever made virtuous or sober by Act of Parliament. It is idle to lecture the public on their artistic shortcomings and tell them to do better. It is only like Mrs Gradgrind telling her children to "*go and be somethingological.*" To be of any value art must be unconscious,

---

[1] *The Tangled Skein*, Sir Reginald Blomfield, R.A.

instinctive ; design should come because you feel it and cannot help putting what you feel into shape. Unless this artistic instinct which was the foundation of all good art in the past can be infused into modern life there is no hope for us. Let us have done with thinking in styles; for let it be understood that the problem we have to solve is not that of reviving this style or that, but of reviving Art itself, which is a very different thing.

Revival of artistic instinct essential

For art really to live it must be vernacular as it was in the Middle Ages, when everyone understood it and practised it as naturally as he spoke his mother-tongue. Now the mass of the people do not care about it or attempt to understand it, and Art will never live again till they do.

Living art must be vernacular

For this indifference of the vulgar to architecture it cannot be denied that the Roman Renaissance is mainly responsible. It made architecture a learned art, not based upon utility but upon the correct use of definite features and proportions, which it needs some knowledge and scholarship to understand. It made it also expensive ; for these necessary features were useless and superfluous, and superfluities can only be afforded by the rich. Architecture therefore became a luxury, and was left to the few who could afford it, and the learned who could understand it.

Renaissance responsible for public indifference

This is of course unnatural; for there is an irrepressible instinct for art inborn in human nature, and to-day we are beginning once more to clamour for decent architecture. And here we have been misled by what I have called the Tyranny of style, to mistake form for principle, and to think that outward features are essential independently of reason. Consequently the popular idea of art at present is ornament; so long as they have plenty of that people are satisfied, and this has lowered the standard of architecture to its present bathos. No doubt good work is

Public mistake of ornament for art

14—5

being done : our best I think infinitely better than what was done fifty or sixty years ago, but our worst is infinitely worse. In the 18th century ugly things were not done : they came when we began to talk about art instead of practising it. Harley Street and Tennyson's "long unlovely street" of Wimpole are not ugly : Russell Square was not ugly till the surveyor put his hideous terra-cotta trimmings round the doors and windows when the building leases fell in. Commonplace if you like, but there is room for commonplace in architecture and it is proper when there is no occasion for anything more. The Rue de Rivoli is commonplace, but it would not be improved by the treatment now being meted out to Upper Regent Street, where monstrosities with domes and polished granite break into Nash's modest stucco. But even when, instead of being like these, hideous, the ornamental features are good in themselves but are inconsistent with the purpose to which they are applied, they become ridiculous and offensive, as for instance at a great store in Oxford Street, London, or a shop at the corner of Broad Street in Oxford, where huge coupled columns rest on insignificant piers below, and the edge of plate glass windows.

True architecture is not a matter of feature or of ornament. It is not a matter of style, or of insistence on certain features, Classic or Gothic, or what not. We are heirs of all past arts but they are for example, and not enslavement. As Michel-Angelo said, "the man who follows others will never go before them ; and he who cannot do well by himself cannot make good use of what has been done by other people." There is a Reason in all good architecture, and it is based on Utility. As Quintilian says, *Nunquam vera species ab utilitate dividitur.* True beauty and utility hang together. That is the clue for our future

Ugly things not done till now

Value of commonplace

Imitation is not art

Reason and Utility the key to good architecture

progress, if we are ever to progress in Art. It was from difficulties of construction, opportunity of material, advantages of better appliances, greater knowledge of nature that the best suggestions came to the architect of the past, and from them they must be derived by the architect of to-day. It is not to the prescriptive formulas of style that we must look for guidance; they are helpful when properly used, fetters when enforced. For growth we must like children have liberty of movement. The question for us is not the battle of Classic or Gothic but that of convention or liberty. There are in truth but two styles of architecture, the BOND and the FREE ; and on our choice between them our future will depend.

FINIS

CHRONOLOGICAL TABLES

DATES OF BUILDINGS

HENRY VI, 1422–61

1433–55	TATTERSALL CASTLE, by Sir Ralph Cromwell. *Feudal fortress*
1455–8	SOUTH WINGFIELD MANOR, by Ralph Lord Cromwell. *Early example of a courtyard house not fortified*
1447–1517	EAST BARSHAM. *Brick with Terra-cotta*
1447–1517	GREAT SNORING RECTORY. *Brick with Terra-cotta*

EDWARD IV, 1461–83. HENRY VII, 1485–1509

1471–83	MUCH WENLOCK. Prior's House. *Gothic*
1475–	GLASTONBURY. The pilgrim's Inn. *Gothic*
1492–	OXFORD. Tower of Magdalen College. *Gothic*
1495–	CANTERBURY CATHEDRAL. Central tower. *Gothic*
1499–	BATH ABBEY. Finished 1616. *Gothic*
1502–	WESTMINSTER. Henry VII's chapel begun. *Gothic*
1506–	WREXHAM. Church Tower finished *Gothic*
1506–	COMPTON WYNYATES, but see 1515–

HENRY VIII, 1509–47

1509–	THE VYNE, by Lord Sandys
1509–	OXFORD. Brasenose College
1510–	CAMBRIDGE. St John's College, Front and Gateway. *Gothic*
1511–	WESTMINSTER. Torrigiano's contract for tomb of Lady Margaret. *Italian Renaissance*
1512–	CAMBRIDGE. King's College, contract for the fan vault, finished 1552
1512–	WESTMINSTER. Torrigiano's contract for Henry VII's tomb. *Italian Renaissance*
1513–7	OXFORD. Corpus Christi College
1514–28	BARRINGTON COURT. *Late Gothic*
1515–20	HAMPTON COURT. First court by Card. Wolsey, finished 1520. Wolsey's Palace finished and surrendered to the King 1526. *Gothic. v. 1530*
1515–20	COMPTON WYNYATES, remodelled by Sir William Compton, begun temp. Henry VII. See 1506–
1515–	LOUTH. Church steeple. *Gothic*
1516–	Dr Young's monument in the Rolls Chapel by Torrigiano. *Italian Renaissance, terra-cotta*
1517–	NEW HALL. Beaulieu. For Henry VIII
1520–5	LAYER MARNEY TOWER. *Late Gothic with Italian detail in Terra-cotta*
1521–7	SUTTON PLACE. *Brick and Terra-cotta. Gothic with Italian details*
1523–5	LAYER MARNEY. The tombs of the Lords Marney. *Marble and Terra-cotta with Italian details*
1525–9	OXFORD. Christchurch Hall for Card. Wolsey. *Gothic*
1525–	FORD ABBEY. Abbot Chard's building. *Gothic with Italian details*
1525–38	HENGRAVE HALL. *Gothic with slight Italian details*
1525	WINCHESTER. *Italian mortuary chests on choir screens*

1526–	HOLBEIN in London. Died of the plague in London in 1543
1530–6	HAMPTON COURT. The Hall by Henry VIII. *Gothic. Pendants of roof Renaissance*
1530–	IL ROSSO engaged at Fontainebleau by Francis I
c. 1530	CHRISTCHURCH, Hants. Lady Salisbury's chantry. *Gothic with Italian arabesques*
1531–	PRIMATICCIO engaged at Fontainebleau by Francis I
1531–5	CAMBRIDGE. King's College organ screen with arms of Anne Boleyn. *Italian arabesques*
1532–41	HENRY VIII's second seal. *Gothic.* v. 1542
1532–	BOXGROVE. Tomb of Lord De-la-Warr. *Terra-cotta*
1533–	ELY. Bishop West's Chapel. *Gothic with Italian details*
1535–	Departure of Benedetto da Rovezzano
1535–6	SKIPTON CASTLE. The long wing by Clifford, Earl of Cumberland
1536–	Suppression of the lesser monasteries
c. 1537–	COWDRAY. Lord Southampton's building. *Traces of Italian detail. Cusping disappeared from windows*
1538–40	Suppression of the larger monasteries
c. 1539–	NONSUCH PALACE. *Gothic with Italian details and figures in stucco*
1542–	HENRY VIII's third seal. *Renaissance,* v. 1532–

EDWARD VI, 1547–53. MARY, 1553–8

1550	JOHN SHUTE, sent to Italy by the Duke of Northumberland
1556	GREAT CRESSINGHAM. Terra-cotta panelling. *Gothic*
1556–64	BURGHLEY HOUSE. East side with Hall and vaulted kitchen on old foundation. v. 1577

ELIZABETH, 1558–1603

1559–	LITTLE MORETON HALL. Half timber (date on oriel)
1560–70	SPEKE HALL. The later work. Half timber
1560–70	LYDGATE HALL. Half timber
1562–8	LOSELY MANOR HOUSE. *Gothic with Renaissance details*
1562–72	LONDON. Middle Temple Hall. *Elizabethan, mixed style*
1563–	THEOBALDS, for Lord Burghley
1565–75	CAMBRIDGE. Gonville and Caius College. Second court by Dr Caius
1566–	LONDON. Royal Exchange, by Sir Thomas Gresham from design by Henry de Pas of Antwerp. *Flemish Renaissance*
1567–79	LONGLEAT, Wilts, for Sir John Thynne
1567–79	KINGSTON HOUSE, Bradford-on-Avon.
1570–5	KIRBY HOUSE, Northants, for Sir Humphrey Stafford
1570–81	GROVE PLACE, Hants, for James Pagett
1572–	CHARLECOTE HOUSE, near Stratford-on-Avon
1572–	EASTBURY HOUSE, Barking
1573	INIGO JONES born
1574	CAMBRIDGE. Caius College. Gate of Honour
1576	HARDWICK HALL, for Elizabeth, Countess of Shrewsbury
1577	LYVEDEN. New building by Sir Thomas Tresham. *Unfinished*
1577	ROTHWELL MARKET HOUSE, by Sir Thomas Tresham. *Unfinished*
1577–87	BURGHLEY HOUSE. Three sides of court and west entrance. Clock-tower dated 1585. North entrance, 1587. v. 1556
1580	Death of PALLADIO

1580–	MONTACUTE HOUSE, for Sir Edward Phelips
1580–8	WOLLATON HALL, for Sir Francis Willoughby, by R. Smythson
1580–8	HOLDENBY HOUSE finished, for Sir Christopher Hatton
1580–90	UPPER SLAUGHTER. Porch with two storeys of Classic pillars
1588	WIMBLEDON HOUSE for Sir Thomas Cecil (destroyed)
1593–5	RUSHTON. Triangular Lodge, by Sir Thomas Tresham
1593–5	COTHELESTONE MANOR. *Square-headed lights, Mullions of attached colonnettes*
1595–	RUSHTON HALL, for Sir Thomas Tresham
1595–	BORWICK HALL. *Light of windows square-headed*
1597–	OXFORD. Duke Humphrey's library refitted and re-roofed by Sir Thomas Bodley
1598–	CAMBRIDGE. S. John's College. Second court by Symons
1600	CAMBRIDGE. S. John's College. Library ceiling by Cobb
1602–	CAMBRIDGE. Trinity College. Fountain in Court: rebuilt 1715

JAMES I, 1603–25

1603–	AUDLEY END
1604–	CAMBRIDGE. Hall of Trinity College
1604–	WESTMINSTER. Queen Elizabeth's tomb by Poutraine alias Colte
1605–8	KNOLE, KENT. Enlarged and remodelled by Thomas Sackville, Earl of Dorset and Lord High Treasurer
1608–	OXFORD. Merton College, new quadrangle
1608–11	HATFIELD HOUSE
1610–3	OXFORD. Wadham College
c. 1610	WIMBLEDON. Eagle House
1612–	YEOVIL. Newton House
1612–	CAMBRIDGE. Nevile's Court at Trinity College
1613–	INIGO JONES'S second visit to Italy
1613–	OXFORD. Quadrangle of Old Schools and Bodleian Library
1616	BATH ABBEY, finished. *Gothic*
1617–	LINCOLN'S INN CHAPEL, by Inigo Jones. *Gothic*
1617–57	GREENWICH. Queen's house by Inigo Jones
1618–35	ASTON HALL for Sir Thomas Holte. *Elizabethan or Jacobean, mixed style*
1619–	LONDON. Banqueting Hall by Inigo Jones. *Pure Palladian Renaissance*
1620–9	OXFORD. Hall of Trinity College. Chapels of Lincoln and Jesus Colleges. *Gothic*

CHARLES I, 1625–49

1625–30	RUSHTON HALL. Front cloister, staircase, etc., added by the Cockaynes
1626	LONDON. York stairs by Nicholas Stone (? design of Inigo Jones)
1630–	OXFORD. Fan tracery ceiling to stairs at Christchurch. *Gothic*
1631–	LONDON. Covent Garden Piazza and St Paul's Church by Inigo Jones
1631–6	OXFORD. S. John's Garden Court
1631–40	LONDON. S. Paul's west front by Inigo Jones
1632	Birth of Sir Christopher Wren
1632–	OXFORD. Gate to Physic Garden by Stone (? design of Inigo Jones)
1637–42	OXFORD. Oriel College. Chapel consecrated 1642
1637–	OXFORD. S. Mary's Church. South porch by Nicholas Stone
1638	CAMBRIDGE. Clare Hall. East front and Entrance

1638	KIRBY. Alterations by Inigo Jones
1638	WINCHESTER. Cathedral Choir Screen by Inigo Jones
1639–40	OXFORD. S. Mary Hall. *Gothic*

COMMONWEALTH, 1649–60

1652	Death of Inigo Jones
1656–	OXFORD. Brasenose College Chapel, consecrated 1666. *Gothic mixed with Classic*
1659–	CAMBRIDGE. Pembroke College. South side of second Court

CHARLES II, 1660–85

1663–	CAMBRIDGE. Pembroke College Chapel by Christopher Wren
1664–	OXFORD. Sheldonian Theatre by Christopher Wren
1675	LONDON. S. Paul's first stone laid
1676–	CAMBRIDGE. Trinity College Library. Sir Christopher Wren
1681–	CHATSWORTH by Talman
1681–	KING'S LYNN. Custom House by Henry Bell
1682–	OXFORD. Tom tower by Wren
1682–92	CHELSEA. Hospital by Wren
1688–	CAMBRIDGE. King's College organ and case

WILLIAM AND MARY, 1689–1702

1689–1700	HAMPTON COURT. The Fountain Court by Wren
1691	OXFORD. Trinity College Chapel by Aldrich and Wren
1696	GREENWICH. Hospital begun by Wren. King Charles's block had been partly built by Webb from Inigo Jones's designs
1701–	CASTLE HOWARD by Vanbrugh

ANNE, 1702–14

1705–	BLENHEIM by Vanbrugh
1710–	LONDON. S. Paul's top stone of lantern fixed
1710–	OXFORD. Queen's College, new quadrangle by Hawksmoor
1711–8	GREENWICH. S. Alphege by Hawksmoor except the steeple
1711–8	OXFORD. Clarendon building by Hawksmoor

GEORGE I, 1714–27

1714–29	LONDON. S. Mary-le-Strand by James Gibbs
1716–19	LONDON. S. Mary, Woolnoth by Hawksmoor
1720–30	LONDON. S. George's, Bloomsbury by Hawksmoor
1721–6	LONDON. S. Martin-in-the-Fields by Gibbs
1722–	CAMBRIDGE. Senate House by Gibbs
1723–	CAMBRIDGE. King's College buildings by Gibbs
1723	Death of Sir Christopher Wren
1725–	BATH. John Wood's plans for laying out the city
1725–	LONDON. Christ Church, Spitalfields, by Hawksmoor
1725–	ETON. College Library

GEORGE II, 1727-60

1737–47	OXFORD. Radcliffe Library by Gibbs
1739–53	LONDON. Mansion House by G. Dance the elder
1750	HORACE WALPOLE at Strawberry Hill. *Neo-Gothic*

GEORGE III, 1760–1820

1760	LONDON. The Admiralty screen by R. Adam
1761–5	KEDDLESTONE by Adam, begun by Paine
1762	STUART'S *Athens*, vol. I. published
1764–7	KENWOOD by Adam
1765	PERCY'S *Reliques of Ancient Poetry*, published
1768	Royal Academy of Arts founded
1770–82	LONDON. Newgate prison by G. Dance the younger
1776	LONDON. Somerset House begun by Sir William Chambers, R.A.
1788	OXFORD. Oriel College Library by James Wyatt
1801	CAMBRIDGE. Downing College by Wilkins
c. 1817	RICKMAN. Published his *Attempt to distinguish the styles of English architecture, from the Conquest to the Reformation*

GEORGE IV, 1820–30

1823–7	CAMBRIDGE. Corpus Christi, buildings by Wilkins. *Neo-Gothic*
1824	CAMBRIDGE. King's College, new buildings, street front by Wilkins. *Neo-Gothic*

INDEX

Printed in U.S.A. by
NOBLE OFFSET PRINTERS, INC.
NEW YORK, N.Y. 10003